To Annie & Eli —
   With many great memories
and much love — and thanks
for a great weekend!
              Andy

The Corsair Years
by Andrew Jones

Turner Publishing Company

Turner Publishing Company

The Front Line of Military History Books
412 Broadway, P.O. Box 3101
Paducah, KY 42002-3101
(502) 443-0121

Author: Andrew Jones

Publisher's Staff:
Robert J. Martin, Chief Editor

Design by Luke Henry, Henry Designs

Library of Congress
Catalog Card No. 95-060329
ISBN: 1-563311-181-0

Printed in the United States of America
Limited Edition

"In our youth ourhearts were touched with fire. It was given us to learn at the outset that life is a profound and passionate thing."

Capt. Oliver Wendell Holmes, Jr.
20th Massachusetts Volunteerrs, 1863

"You can always tell a fighter pilot, but you can't tell him much."

Hoary old bromide of more wit than validity

For Friends who failed to return

Preface

I first met Andy Jones in 1969 while I was serving as Military Assistant to General Lewis W. Walt, one of the greatest combat leaders in the history of The United States Marine Corps. Andy was then a writer-editor at *The Reader's Digest*, and he was writing an in-depth article about the battle for Khe Sahn in Vietnam. While those of us who were associated with him at the time knew he had been a Marine aviator during World War II, none of us realized the extent of his combat service. The author is a member of a unique generation of Americans — a self-effacing generation that marched off to fight what was to be the war to end all wars and, victorious in battle, quietly came back to their well-earned place in society. They asked for little in return after giving so much.

And so it is that, some fifty years later, Andrew Jones, now retired and "deeply grieved by the seemingly endless flareups of savagery and suffering around the globe," takes time out from his service as a Hospice volunteer and singing bass in his church choir to look back upon his years as a Marine fighter pilot during "The Great War." After reading *The Corsair Years* one will be reminded of the comment from *The Bridges of Toko-Ri*: "Lord, where do we get such men?"

The author begins with a scene familiar to those of us old enough to remember the start of World War II — a father standing alone on a sidewalk in New York City waving farewell to a son who is embarking on a journey which will eventually put him in harm's way. He then unfolds a warm and poignant story of a love affair between men and a machine, between the Marines who flew it and the F4U Corsair. Many Marines believed from their first flight in one that the Corsair had a heart and a soul of its own. History has proved them right.

In Andy's words, this story is "a collection of reminiscinces, a farrago of joys, sorrows, victories and defeats that gets dredged up every year at our reunions." In reality, however, it is far more than that: it's a personal story of Marines in combat written by a combat Marine. As one who spent thirty-seven years of his adult life in the service of his country, I commend *The Corsair Years* to all Americans. It is a book replete with values, patriotism, courage, and selfless dedication to God, to country, and to fellow Marines. Captain Jones has given all Americans, particularly Marines, a clear definition of the phrase *Semper Fidelis — Always Faithful!*

Paul X. Kelley
General, U.S. Marine Corps (Ret.)
28th Commandant of The Marine Corps

Introduction

Out of the blue some years ago my son Seaver said to me, "Dad, you were lucky — you had a war. "

Lucky? The word seemed an odd choice. It soon came clear, though, that he was more concerned with his own life situation than my supposed good fortune in having been of service age during World War II. He was expressing a 16-year-old's difficulties in coming to grips with the adult community; he was telling me I had it easy, I had adulthood jammed down my throat, everything laid out for me, I had only to listen to my superiors and follow orders. He was trying to say that he was not so lucky as I.

He mentioned a story I'd told him about an accident that occurred one morning in November, 1943, while our Marine fighter squadron was in the Hawaiian Islands preparing to go south into the Pacific combat area. Several of us had gathered in the doorway of our readyroom to watch a replacement pilot fresh out of Stateside training take off for his first hop in one of our F4U Corsairs. The sights, sounds and details of that moment remain indelibly in mind — a poker game at the table in the room behind us, a radio announcer reporting scores of high school football games, the drifty laughter and chidings of crewmen and mechanics at their flightline duties along the tarmac . . .

We knew no more about this new pilot than his name, but he looked confident enough as he walked out to the plane, strapped himself into the cockpit, fired up the engine and taxied out to the runway. Our early model Corsairs had engine torque problems that caused the left wing to drop on takeoff — it was a tendency which, if not instantly corrected by applying hard right rudder, could swerve the plane off the runway and into bad trouble — and standing in the readyroom door that morning we watched it happen; the plane's wheels lifted off the concrete, its left wing dipped low, the pilot lost control and we suddenly found ourselves staring at a Pratt & Whitney R 2800 engine coming straight at us. Somebody yelled, "HIT THE DECK!" and we all pitched forward, heads down into the dirt.

Miraculously, the plane missed our building by a few feet but it demolished the squadron head (latrine) across the road — we looked up in time to see its left wing slash through the wooden shack, taking away its roof and walls as neatly as a cleaver slicing bologna. The wingtip had clipped the water main off at the ground and a silver fountain of crystal clear water was soaring into the air. The plane finally thrashed to a stop in a cane field, the canopy flew open and the pilot jumped out, dazed but unharmed.

We were treated then to an extraordinary sight — we saw a dust-swathed figure, one of our armorers from the ordnance shop, rise up suddenly amid the waist-high piles of kindling which were all that remained of the head. If he'd been standing erect at the moment of impact he would have been cut in half, but he'd been enjoying one of the simple pleasures of the poor and now, drenching in the water main shower bath and clearly stunned out of his wits, he kicked his trousers from his ankles and started running up the road, naked below the plimsoll line, as fast as his legs would carry him.

Seaver hooted in glee at this image until I told him what we saw next — a group of men standing around a body in the road. We ran over. One of our squadron corpsmen had been struck by the plane's undercarriage. He lay on his broken back, his ashen face turned to the sky. He was dead.

The guffaws ceased, eyes sought mine as though expecting an explanation of this too-abrupt turn of narrative events. There was none, of course. I shrugged. "That's the way things happened sometimes," I said lamely, "farce and tragedy all in the same breath. You never knew what was coming next."

I recall my son's bewilderment as he tried to absorb this yin and yang of the inexplicable, comedy and heartbreak commingled simultaneously half way around a world he knew little about a decade before he was born, and I know now that his assertion that I was lucky to have been a party to such experiences at his age has more truth than I had thought — trauma is a teacher as effective as it is terrible, and to learn early that life and death often go arm-in-arm could very well catapult an impressionable stripling into something like adulthood in a hurry. It might also explain, at least in part, why we who lived and flew together for three wartime years still meet annually in cities around the country to hash them over.

These reminiscences cover wide territory, personal and collective, emotional and historical, befitting a time which now seems completely set apart from anything we have known before or since. For factual accuracy I have referred to the histories of Samuel Eliot Morison, Walter Karig and Robert Sherrod and I've consulted official records in Marine Corps archives; for their informative content and wider perspectives I have drawn on a number of related popular sources, notably Barrett Tillman's Corsair, J. Robert Moskin's The U.S. Marine Corps Story, and Eric Larrabee's Commander in Chief: Franklin Delano Roosevelt's Lieutenants, and Their War.

But the main effort throughout these pages has been to recapture and present a close-in depiction of World War II as experienced by me and those with whom I served. Real people appear and reappear — and disappear forever — according to the record carved in memory's hardest rock. My father stands alone on the sidewalk outside 120 Broadway in New York City waving goodbye to his son driving off in a bus for pre-flight school. My sandlot baseball player friend Chick Whalen is forced to ditch his Corsair in the Pacific during a storm, finds he can no longer fly over water and is sent home. Jack Butler, a school and college classmate, is hit while strafing a Japanese gun position and obliterates it and himself by flying into it wide open. Our ordnance crewmen assemble bomb racks from scrap metal and turn us into one of America's first fighter-bomber squadrons while one of them, a young corporal from New York named Art Buchwald, begins a career in journalism by putting together our weekly squadron newspaper.

The story is, to repeat, a collection of reminiscences, a farrago of joys, sorrows, victories and defeats that gets dredged up every year at our reunions. We're in our 60s and 70s now, our glass-in-hand recollections are fallible, but invariably Jack Dufford or Ken Geelhood or Jim Bathrick suddenly breaks up and says, "Hey, remember the morning that guy flew through the shithouse?" Sure we remember (we incline to forget our dead corpsman in the road) and we know that those of us who survived this and other occurrances recounted herein are indeed lucky.

One thing more we know: it is that our youthful World War II years comprise the hinge experience of our lives, and they will be with us for good or ill as long as we draw breath.

Part One
The Beast

Chapter One

It is a hot, windless North Florida noon at Lee Field, an outlying base of Jacksonville Naval Air Station, in May, 1943. Marine second lieutenants Bill Degan, Chick Whalen and I have just landed our F4F Grumman Wildcat fighter planes, old patched-up war-wearies which months before had been shooting down Japanese aircraft over Guadalcanal and were now serving as operational trainers for fledgeling Navy and Marine fighter pilots. At that moment we're on our way to the mess hall for lunch. Suddenly Degan stops and points at a plane on final approach into the field, dropping wheels and flaps as it swoops toward the head of the runway.

We recognize it instantly from photographs in aircraft recognition classes but we've never seen a real one before — with its long blue-gray snout, inverted gull wings and gangly landing gear it looks like nothing so much as a huge snarly hornet coming down to sting hell out of whatever it finds under its feet. It settles on the tar with a screech, its tires leave little white puffs of burnt rubber at the point of contact. Gradually it slows, slows, slows almost to a stop, then turns off onto a taxi strip and comes thundering back toward the maintenance hanger. A mechanic waits to give it parking directions. Following his hand signals, it swings in a majestic circle and switches off a hundred feet from where we stand gawking.

Chick breaks our silence with a long, low whistle. We're looking at an F4U Chance-Vought Corsair, an aircraft as new to the U.S. military inventory as are the three of us. Its Hamilton Standard three-bladed propeller whines down to rest, its enormous engine clinks and clanks as it begins to cool, the pilot climbs from the cockpit to the wing and steps to the ground. We study him head to toe — tall, slightly stooped, an older man, doesn't look military but wearing Navy summer issue helmet and flight suit. As he slings his chute up on the wing, our Lee Field C.O. and half a dozen top station brass come hurrying out of the hangar, crowd around him, shake his hand, engulf him in enthusiastic greeting . . .

We stare at each other. Who is he? Must be somebody important.

"*Important?* Bet your ass he's important — anybody who flies this airplane must be first cousin to God!"

Finally we turn away from the scene and walk to the mess hall where we learn from table scuttlebutt that the lanky visitor is, indeed, practically blood kin to deity — he's none other than Charles Lindbergh, "Lucky Lindy," the Lone Eagle of the Atlantic, who had offered his services as a civilian consultant to Chance-Vought and other aircraft manufacturers. The word going around is that he'd had much to do with the design and development of the bent-wing fighter he'd just flown down from the factory in Connecticut.

Since we student pilot were told nothing that did not serve to hustle us through our final stage of training and out to combat squadrons waiting for us, the arrival of a Corsair in our midst spawned rumors like weevils in new cotton. A notice posted on our ready room bulletin board in late afternoon only added to the confusion. It read:

> All Marine students aboard the station
> will have a one-hour familiarization
> flight in the F4U before completing the
> training syllabus.

We crowded around it, questions tumbling in a noisy babble . . .
"What the hell, aren't us Navy guys going to fly it too?"
"Guess not."
"Why not? It's a Navy plane, isn't it?"
"Dunno. They say it's too hot for carrier operations."
"Too hot for — you mean? . . ."
"Sure, that's what the Man's telling us. It's not a Navy plane, it's for us gyrenes flying off terra firma. It's a *Marine* plane."

And so it was. The one that landed in our midst that noon was the first operational model, the F4U-1, known as the "Birdcage U" because of its segmented cockpit canopy. Later models were equipped with single-piece perspex "bubble" canopies, raised tail wheels, four-bladed propellers and other improvements, and before the war ended, when Navy, Marine, British, Canadian, New Zealand and Australian pilots were flying them off carriers as well as land bases, the Chance-Vought Corsair was acclaimed by allied and enemy airmen (the latter in post-war interrogations) the most versatile and effective fighter-bomber aircraft in the Pacific theater and probably any other. But it was always thought of as a "Marine" plane; from its first appearance in the headlines to the present, public opinion has fixed on it as the workhorse of Marines in Pacific islands, the glamor steed of Marine aerial aces, and the pride, muscle and backbone of Marine Corps aviation in World War II.

By this time Chick, Bill and I had been together most of the eleven months since June of 1942 when we entered pre-flight school at the University of North Carolina in Chapel Hill. After pre-flight came elementary flight training, 40 hours in the old "yellow peril" biplanes, stalls and stunts, landings and takeoffs and our first taste of night flying and holding position in formation. Degan and Whalen took elementary at Naval Air Station Squantum in Massachusetts, home country for them. I was sent to NAS Ponchartrain in New Orleans. But we were together again when, the week before Thanksgiving, we arrived at Pensacola to begin intermediate and advance flight training.

Compared to what had gone before, Pensacola was big time. For one thing, we were done with fabric biplanes and into all- metal low-wing monoplanes — formation flying in "Vultee Vibrators" followed by instrument instruction in the North American SNJ, known to the Army as the AT 6. Also, we enjoyed a social upgrading; we were now fullfledged aviation cadets, we had Officers Club privileges and we were regarded by our superiors, somewhat tentatively, as men of the world.

Evidence of this last was brought home to us during a lecture by a medical staff officer who began by flashing on the auditorium screen a photograph of a naked male body in the final stages of tertiary syphilis. Warming to his subject, he showed us photos of shankered penises, the ravages of gonhorrea, the whole revolting gamut of venereal infection. Pensacola, he told us with undisguised clinical enthusiasm, boasted the highest per capita VD rate of any city in the country. He concluded by snapping on the ceiling lights and leering balefully down at us. "I leave you gentlemen with an old medical adage," he intoned. "Flies breed germs — keep yours closed."

I recall another auditorium lecture, memorable for its consequences. It was a presentation on chemical warfare by a slight, intense, balding Navy officer a few years older than ourselves. He looked familiar to me, and while he was demonstrating the uses of a standard issue gas mask I suddenly placed him. "Hey Dege," I whispered to Bill beside me, "I know this guy. He dated my sister a couple of summers ago!" I remembered him as a dashing figure, a sailor and athlete; I was happy to have discovered a friend in high places, and when he'd finished his spiel I dashed up on stage and introduced myself.

Lt. Newton "Buddy" Buckner looked me over, and as we shook hands I thought I detected a malefic glint in his eyes. "We have an outdoor demonstration tomorrow at 1300, Cadet Jones," he said. "You'll be there, will you?"

"Sure, Buddy — ah, *Sir*!" I replied.

The demonstration was held beside a tent in a field near the Squadron Three hangar. Two dozen of us newly arrived cadets were issued gas masks; we tried them on, took them off. "It's my experience," Lt. Buckner said, "that there's an individual in every class who fails to take my message as seriously as he might. Now we're going to see what happens to him when he's slow to don his mask during a gas attack. I'll ask Cadet Jones to step forward." I stepped forward. Lt. Buckner took the mask from my hand, produced a tear gas cannister, popped it and tossed it into the tent. "Cadet Jones," he ordered, "you will walk through the tent and come out the other side — and I suggest you be quick about it."

I was not quick enough — half way through I felt as though someone had hit me in the chest with a sledge hammer; my throat seized tight, I was blinded by tears, I stumbled out the far side and fell on my face. Sitting up, gasping for air, I could see my fellow cadets had been impressed by my experience and had absorbed the intended lesson.

I had learned a lesson too, but it had less to do with gas attacks than with thinking twice in future before chumming up to senior officers.

During instrument training at Pensacola we were offered two choices which would determine our future military careers: what type aircraft we wanted to fly and which of the two services we hoped to join upon graduation ("hoped" is the right word; there was no guarantee of compliance in either case). My leaning toward the Marines probably began in my father's library where as a boy I pored over Col. John Tomason's books and pencil sketches of Marine campaigns in France in 1918. And there was another more imminent incitement: it went by the name of a nasty malarial lump of jungle in the Solomon Islands.

At this time the battle for Guadalcanal, code-named "Cactus", was at its height. Six months before, our carrier air groups, augmented by a handful of Marines in outmoded planes based on Midway, had sunk four Japanese carriers, cracking the spine of Imperial seapower. In August, two months later, the Marine 1st Division landed on Guadalcanal and, digging in, had begun the process of turning the Japanese tide of expansion southward toward Australia back toward the homeland. Guadalcanal was the geographical turning point in the Pacific; it was where we told the Japs *aqui no mas* — this far and no further — and in ground shool we were reading combat debriefings of Marine fighter pilots, each one ten feet tall, defending Henderson Field (named for Maj. Lofton R. Henderson who was killed leading the Midway dive bombers). Guadalcanal looked like the kind of action the three of us wanted; we decided we would fly fighter type aircraft and, when the Big Day arrived, pin our wings of gold on Marine Corps green.

All went accordingly. We took advance fighter training in SNJs, graduated as Marine 2nd lieutenants on April 6, 1943, and reported across the state to Lee Field where we commenced operational training in the very planes we'd been reading about — the Grumman Wildcat I'd flown that May morning had seven Jap meatballs pasted on its fuselage beneath the cockpit. But change was in the wind: the arrival of a Corsair at our facility and a bulletin announcing we were to check out in it could only mean that a new evolution in Marine aviation was underway and we would be part of it.

That night after supper several of us went to the maintenance hangar for a closer inspection. The plane cut a sinister figure in the shadows with its snout angling up toward the rafter lights — surrounded by stubby little Grummans in various stages of engine repair, it suggested a winged creature from outer space that had chewed the engine cowlings off its lesser brethren and eaten its fill. We walked around it, we ran fingers over its taped gunports, someone kicked a tire. Completing our circuit, we stood in silence staring up at its 13-foot canoe-paddle propellor blades ...

I was as awed as the others but there was more to it for me than the impact of its physical presence; I was gripped by a premonition that derived from an early childhood memory of standing chin-high at a New York hotel window gazing down on bands playing and ant-sized people marching along Fifth Avenue in a blizzard of confetti — my father was directing my attention to a man who'd just flown across the ocean riding beside the president or the mayor or somebody in the back of an open limousine. Now, staring up at this great walloping monster of an airplane fourteen years later, I found it easy to let memory take precedence over immediate impression, to grease the skids of imagination and let it slide full throttle into fantasy — I was ready to believe that Charles Lindbergh had flown this machine here today because he knew it had my name on it, because he'd known all along that it was destined to join forces with that kid in the hotel window some day and do great things with him —

I was interrupted in mid-flight by someone knocking over a ladder — it fell to the concrete floor with a crash that echoed throughout the tin hangar like the crack of doom.

The spell was broken, talk resumed, we all started shuffling toward the hangar door. I forget which of us turned back for a parting look and summarized our impressions in three words: "What a beast!"

We laughed, but the name stuck. Thereafter the Corsair was known to us as "The Beast."

In the next week we studied the operations manual, we memorized its performance characteristics and logged on-the-deck cockpit time until we could lay hands on all switches and controls with our eyes closed. Big and powerful beyond any fighter ever built, the six-ton F4U's Double Wasp radial engine, rated at 2000 horsepower, delivered a climbing capability of 3000 feet per minute, a maximum level flight speed of 360 knots at 20,000 feet and a ceiling of over 35,000. It was armed with six .50 caliber Browning air-cooled machine guns, three in each wing, all trajectories boresighted to converge at a single point 300 yards in front of the flight path — hit it at boresight range and you could shoot down a flying battleship.

The Beast was America's answer to the Japanese Zero fighter which at Midway and since had proved itself superior to our Grummans in speed, rate of climb and maneuverability. With it we were embarking on a whole new theory of fighter tactics known as hit-and-run. No more dogfighting, we were told — if you try to dogfight a Zero he'll turn inside you and shoot your tail off. What you do with the Corsair is drop on him or climb up to him, kill him with a single burst, then dive away. The lightweight Zero has the maneuverability edge but you've got the speed, rate of climb and firepower. Use them.

This was all ground drill and blackboard instruction. It was not until we'd completed the training syllabus that Cdr. Noel Bacon, a veteran Flying Tiger of Chennault's American Volunteer Group in China and presently our operational instructor, sent us out to the flightline one after another to take it into the air.

The delay proved sound because things happened in the interim to sharpen our skills and add to our overall flying experience. One afternoon as we were returning from a gunnery hop off the coast near St. Augustine, Bill Degan's engine quit and he was forced to make a wheels-up landing in the Atlantic. He did a beautiful job. Dege, a big blue-eyed, slope- shouldered, hawk-nosed South Boston Irishman, was a former Boston College football star and a competition swimmer and, circling him at two hundred feet, we watched him jump out, inflate his life raft, climb in and wave up at us. Cdr. Bacon radioed the St. Augustine crash boat and we stayed in our circle to mark his position until it arrived. Meanwhile Dege, paddling happily around in a school of porpoises, had shown us how to do something any of us might have to do any moment.

It's said that engine failures occur in series and, sure enough, a few days later while we had our Grummans in a strafing pattern at two thousand feet over Palatka swampland I had a frantic call from Chick Whalen behind me saying I was on fire. I looked in the rear vision mirror and beheld a black, smoke-like ribbon trailing in my wake. A glance at the instrument panel told me it wasn't smoke, I wasn't on fire — the needle of my oil pressure gauge was dropping toward zero, indicating that an oil line had ruptured and my engine was seizing up. I nosed over instantly to keep gliding speed. Since I had already lost enough altitude to make a parachute bailout risky, I started searching for solid ground below on which to put an old worn out Wildcat that was about to end a distinguished Pacific career in a Florida marsh.

I spotted a plowed field that I could reach without stretching my glide, flung the canopy back, dropped flaps and, thinking about landing in loose earth instead of on tar, kept the wheels retracted. The approach was over a post and rail fence; at fifty feet I levelled off and dropped in. I hit hard but smoothly, showering dirt out ahead of the cowl, then slewed slightly to the left and came to a stop — though I hadn't yet done it, I imagined it must have been much like catching the second or third wire on a carrier deck.

Scrambling out of the cockpit I saw a mule at the far end of the field galloping away with a plow flopping along behind it. Off to my right, two bulging white eyeballs in a black face stared at me from behind a tree. I jumped down off the wing and beckoned to the man. He came slowly, terrified — obviously his plowing had been interrupted when he'd looked over his shoulder, saw this thing coming at him from the sky, whacked his mule on its south end and run for cover. I went to meet him. He stopped, still ogling me in terror. "M-Mistuh," he stammered, "is you a J-J-Jap?"

I reassured him as best I could and asked if there was a phone nearby. He pointed to a house beyond a soybean field. I walked to the house, called Lee Field operations and reported my location and circumstances, saying I was okay except for some mean-tempered redbugs that had gotten inside my flight suit and were trying to chew my legs off.

This episode had a rather serendipitous beginning and end. The beginning had occurred a month before when spring rains washed out a railroad bridge near Brunswick, Georgia, stranding two Navy nurses on their way by train to duty at our Lee Field sickbay. Two of us were dispatched in SNJs to pick them up at NAS Brunswick and fly them aboard.

As in the fairy tale, there was a pretty one and a fat one. My flight mate landed first and got the looker, leaving me to pry the corpulent number into my back seat. We took off and all went well until, half way home, we were jumped by a P-51 from a nearby Army base. Tactical workouts with the Army whenever we met up was regular procedure, and without a thought I turned toward my attacker and joined battle. I slipped under his first pass but, as I was in a training plane and he was flying a fighter, I had to do a lot of violent splitting and rolling, cutting hard right and left, diving down among the mangroves and up again to prevent him from bringing his guns to bear on me. Suddenly I remembered my passenger — in the mirror I saw the poor woman slumped comatose in her seat. I waggled my wings and broke off.

Back at the field two ground crewmen and I pried her out and onto the ground. She opened her eyes, breathed deeply, glared at me and, yanking at her skirt, gasped, "Don't get sick, Sonny. If I ever catch you in one of our hospital beds I'll *kill* you!"

It happened that my Palatka redbug bites became infected and the day after the crash landing I reported to sickbay. While I waited in the receiving room a deep female voice boomed behind me in the doorway: "Well, *well*, look who we have *here*!" I cringed, peering slowly around. She was smiling. She'd gotten over her mad and was ready to josh about her back seat ride down the coast. While we were thus engaged this tender- handed Florence Nightingale treated my redbug wounds and sent me away a well man.

About this time, too, Vallory Willis, my girl from civilian days, came down from New York for a visit. It started as a disaster. I had reserved a room for her at a nearby hotel and I drove the dozen miles in to Jacksonville to meet her one o'clock train. The train, it turned out, was in two sections - - she was on the second, due to arrive four hours later. I returned to the field for a tactics flight at two o'clock which would leave me plenty of time to get back to the railroad station to meet her, but when our flight landed shortly after three we found the base on scramble alert. Our none-too-reliable radar was picking up unidentified aircraft a hundred miles at sea and closing the coastline; all planes were armed, pilots in their cockpits and crewmen standing by to start engines. Of course the thought of an air attack on the Florida coast occasioned raucous hilarity along the flight line ("Hot damn, I'm gonna bag me a coupla Messerschmitts off those carriers the Germans got so many of!") but I took no part in the fun — I had visions of a disenchanted Miss Willis boarding the next train back to New York.

The alert was cancelled at sunset and I found her in her hotel room, tired and famished but understanding. I recall our meeting that evening with poignance for we'd shared many good times over the years; being with her brought back memories of summer beach parties on Martha's Vineyard, faces of friends around driftwood bonfires, voices singing "Aura Lee" and "I've Been Working on the Railroad". But we'd seen little of each other recently and our romance had cooled — we both knew it, we both felt it, and we understood what this meeting was about: it was to discover whether our feelings for each other had indeed burned themselves out.

They had. When I handed Val up into her northbound Pullman

two days later we parted with the unspoken knowledge that we'd tumbled into and out of a near-terminal case of puppy love and it was time for us to go fondly our separate ways.

I think that from the day the F4U appeared at Lee Field most Marines of the training detachment started measuring time against the hour they'd climb into it, sign the yellow sheet and fire it up. My turn came at two o'clock on our last afternoon aboard. I lugged my parachute out to the Beast under a clear sky with scattered cumulus — light easterly breeze, visibility all the way to Portugal, the best of flying conditions. Slinging the chute up on the wing and doing the customary walk-around inspection of propellor and fuselage for dents and fluid leaks, I could feel the eyes of the plane crew silently following my every move . . .

As noted, the Corsair squatting at night in a hangar gave rise to fanciful impressions. Buckling into its cockpit, however, impressions were strictly practical and even more daunting. The first were of height — how far it was down to concrete — and of the stubbiness and seeming inadequacy of its wings. Then, with the pop of the starter cartridge and the vibration of its engine turning over at idle, it underwent a character change; it took on the liveliness of a creature born for the air and anxious to be into it.

I've relived this first flight over and over ever since. Taxiing out to the strip is a matter of nervously kicking the tail from side to side to see around that Godawful long nose aimed at the clouds. More nervousness going down the checkoff list — trim tab settings, cowl flaps, instrument readings, testing the magnetos by firewalling the throttle, thundering the engine while hugging the stick into the crotch and twisting the mag switch — right, left, back to both.

Finally, words that have been rehearsed a hundred times in imagination are spoken aloud into the hand mike: "Corsair to tower, request takeoff permission."

The laconic reply: "Roger Corsair, clear for takeoff."

Gunning the engine, swinging out onto the strip, lining up with the runway. Full brakes, full throttle again. One last glance around — Cdr. Bacon high on the control tower's observation platform watching, mechanics and crewmen standing motionless along the flightline, all watching. A momentary flash of panic: *son-of-a-bitch, the whole base is watching* — what am I *doing* out here in this thing?

Followed by a deep breath. Well, okay, here we go . . .

Suddenly there's no more thinking, no more nervousness, just concentration, reflex hands and feet, eyes fixed on black tar centered by a white line disappearing faster and faster under the nose. Little forward stick, get the tail up. Okay. Right rudder against torque. Good. Now back, b-a-a-ck on the stick, easy does it, that's it ... St-e-a-d-y-y ......

Hey, look at this, we're off the ground! My God, *we're off!*

Thinking again. Retract wheels (Cu-*clump*), close canopy (Ka-*BLOOM*), ease throttle, let her gain speed. Speed? Hell, this bucket doesn't know anything *but* speed, not bumblebee speed like the stubby little Grummans but big roaring bird speed like a ... yes, in a left wingover out of the traffic pattern like this, like an eagle, a swooper and soarer ... and now, levelling off at angels five, like a big sea bird going flat our downwind, an albatross with a gale under its tail . . .

We bank and turn east, out over the Atlantic — looking down, the sea appears a sheet of molten steel moving in horizon-wide slow motion, massively wrinkled and webbed with white wisps of foam; looking level, the baby blue zenith lightens to silver as it curves down and melts into the nacreous mist around the edge of visibility. And here, hanging seemingly motionless in the sky's very center, the Corsair is in its element, the groundling Beast becomes airborne Beauty; buttoned up tight and roaring along straight and level, it's the way it's designer and engineers envisioned it; to the pilot at its controls, it's the mighty metal warhorse of his imagination, responsive to the slightest pressure, as willing and subservient as Alexander's Bucephalus charging the Persians . . .

On sudden impulse, looking up at scattered cottonball clouds a thousand feet above, I push over into a dive (not in the flight plan, not supposed to do this, maybe, but what the hell) and as the airspeed needle climbs around the gauge I pull the stick back into a soaring loop, up through the clouds, up and over, slowing to stillness, engine humming upside down above them — body weight hanging in shoulder straps and safety belt, radio cord flapping up, grit from the cockpit well flittering against face and goggles — then easing the stick into neutral, letting the big nose drop straight down through the cloud level, head on for the ocean, rising up again into straight and level flight, tearing the sky apart at close to red-line speed . . .

Well now, how about *that*! What shall we try next, baby?

In such moments of pure exhilaration it was hard to think of the Corsair as a war machine — it felt more like a powerful toy with nothing to do but cavort around the empyrean. There was danger in this, of course; once you got used to the F4U, the tendency was to get casual with it, a mistake some of our number learned the hard way a month later in California. No, it was not a toy; it was a deadly serious piece of equipment; warmaking was it's bottom-line function, it had a job to do in the Pacific, and out there we learned it was not only beautiful to fly but as tough as a fifty cent steak. "Whistling Death," as the Japs called it, dished out destruction in awesome doses and it could remain airworthy after absorbing incredible punishment. I believe that those of us who rejoiced to fly it did so because, consciously or not, we recognized a thoroughly honest vehicle. We knew it as a rock-solid gun platform which, shot full of holes, would bring us home when by rights we should have ended up taking a bath.

Chick was the last of our group to fly it that afternoon and I joined Noel Bacon on the tower observation deck to watch him land. We both tensed at his approach — turning from base leg to final he came in hot, and when he hit the tar he bounced high and wobbly, dropped, bounced again. It was a bad few seconds, but he finally got it settled, rolling straight and slowing down.

Noel's relief was palpable; as of that moment he'd led his banties safely through training, he'd given us all he could of his own expertise, he'd written our orders — carrier checkout at NAS Glenview, a week's leave, then out to Corsair squadrons forming on the West Coast. As Chick taxied back to the flightline he turned to me. He was a quiet man, thoughtful, observing, formal in speech and manner. "You had a good time up there, I gather?" he said in his nasal twang with just the trace of a grin about his lips. It was less a question than an observation — he'd pegged me for a try-anything experimenter in the air and he suspected I'd taken aerobatic liberties.

"Yes Sir, I sure did," I replied.

The grin widened to a smile and he used my Christian name for the first time in six weeks. "You're a fighter type enthusiast, Andrew," he said. "You'll do okay." He stuck out his hand and we shook. "Good luck."

Chapter Two

I'd never in my twenty-one years been farther west than Pittsburgh and the "West Coast" was to me a figment, a Disneyesque never-never land full of flashy cars, palm trees and beaches festooned with busty naiads all bucking for stardom at Warner Brothers. During leave, spent with my father and step-mother at their New York apartment, I'd fast-talked an airline ticket agent into a seat aboard an evening flight out of La Guardia (even travelling under military orders airline reservations in those days were scarce as honest politicians) and I woke the next morning to look down on a splendrous vista of Rocky Mountains, their high passes and couloirs packed with snow — the backbone of the continent in dawn's early light with flanks gleaming pink and lavender and crowned by gray- black peaks. Gazing down on the panorama, cramped against the window and half-asleep, I fell to pondering a close call I'd had ten days earlier during our brief tour at NAS Glenview on the western shore of Lake Michigan.

The morning of our first day aboard was devoted to touch- and-go "bounce drill" in Grummans, practising carrier landings on a country club golf course. A stretch of fairway had been blocked out with sand bags to simulate a carrier deck, in the near left-hand corner of which stood our landing signal officer. One at a time we entered the landing pattern and adjusted our approach in response to his paddle signals — high, low, too fast, too slow. When he slashed at his throat with the inboard paddle we cut throttle, hit the sod in a jarring three-point stall, bounced into the air, poured on power and started around the flight pattern again.

That afternoon our LSO, a Navy lieutenant commander, briefed us for our flight the following morning. This would be the real thing — landing aboard the USS *Wolverine*, a onetime Great Lakes cruise liner converted to an aircraft carrier training ship. We would rendezvous with her out on the Lake and shoot four landings and take-offs, after which we would be considered qualified for carrier operations.

"I want to impress on you the importance of removing your hand from the throttle when I give you the cut," the commander said in closing. "If you don't, your hand will obey Newton's inertial law; it will keep going when the arresting wire yanks you and your plane to a stop, you'll tip forward at full power and chew the flight deck up with your propeller — and, I might add, cause a number of people on board to become very upset. I repeat, get your hand away from the throttle at the cut. Put it up on the wind screen, put it in your pocket, stick it in your ear — I don't care what you do with it so long as you keep it away from the throttle." He donned his cap and walked to the door. "See you tomorrow," he said, and left the room.

He didn't see us tomorrow. A fog bank rolled in that night and shut down flight operations for two days. We played poker and fretted around the station. On the third evening all carrier qualification pilots were invited to a party at the home of a couple in Winnetka, a pleasant affair enlivened by a bevy of local debutantes, but the fog was dissipating and the three of us were too keyed up by prospects of clear weather in the morning to relax and enjoy it.

Conditions were perfect at breakfast time. We took off at 0900, made radio contact with *Wolverine* and found her in the middle of the Lake steaming into a moderate northerly wind. I was first in the formation as we passed over the ship at angels one. I waggled my wings, broke away to the left, enriched fuel mixture and slid the propeller into low pitch. On the downwind leg I dropped tail hook, wheels and flaps, shoved the cockpit canopy back into the locked-open position and began my approach around and down toward the ship's stern, eyes on the LSO and his paddles. He was giving me the come-on, flight path fine, everything in the groove. As I crossed the stern, nose high, his paddle swung up for the cut. I pulled back the throttle and, as instructed, took my left hand from it and raised it to grip the edge of the wind screen.

Then, responding to some urging incomprehensible short of divine guidance — thinking of it looking down at the Colorado Rockies that June morning broke me into a sweat —I took my hand from the screen. A split second later I hit the flight deck, caught the arresting wire and jerked to a stop, whereupon the cockpit canopy obeyed Newton's inertial law by flying forward and slamming shut with a resounding *CLANG!* It had failed to lock open, and if I'd held onto the wind screen it would have chopped my hand off at the thumb joint.

The next few seconds are a mnemonic jumble. I caught a glimpse of the LSO's ashen face across the deck — he'd seen it all, he understood what had happened and my mental turmoil at the moment, but the second plane was already in its approach and he had to clear the flight deck for it. The instant the crewmen disengaged the wire from my tail hook he motioned me to take off. I acted again without thinking — I raised hook and flaps, gunned the engine to full power, charged down the deck, off the bow and into the air. . .

We completed the exercise without further mishap but, still staring down at the mountains, I wondered where I would be now if things had gone the other way on that first landing. I was left-handed — what would the rest of my life have been without it? Not much, so far as I could see. I'd completed sophomore year at Princeton University before pre-flight, I'd probably go back and take my diploma. I'd played football, boxed, and stroked the freshman crew. I was no scholar, though, and my gridiron and sweep-swinging days would be over. I loved music, but I could not have gone on with the piano. I thought of my Dad. Mother had died before the war, that fall he'd married a wonderful widow with children the age of his own and they'd visited me in Pensacola on their honeymoon. I had to smile at this recollection. Dad strode out on the flightline wearing a gray Homburg hat, polo coat and business suit (Laura's pet name for him was "Mr. New England"), and without a word he'd climbed up on the wing of an SNJ, studied the cockpit and instrument panel, then stepped down to confront his youngest, the wet-behind-the-ears baby of the family. "Do you really fly this thing?" he asked incredulously. "No, Pop," I said, "I just go along for the ride. It flies me. . ."

I laughed aloud then, and the man drinking orange juice in the next seat turned and grinned at me. I grinned back. I looked down at my left hand and spread my fingers. Well, I thought, it didn't happen — I still have the damn thing and it's working fine.

My flight landed on schedule at Los Angeles and I took a bus down the coast to Marine Corps Air Station Miramar in the hills east of San Diego. Dege, Chick and Curly Lehnert, another of our group from pre-flight days, had already arrived, and that afternoon we reported to the base commander's office to receive our squadron assignments. Chick and Curley were ordered to a squadron forming at Santa Barbara, Dege and I to another at El Toro.

It was a disappointment for we hoped we'd all be sent to the same outfit, but orders were orders and that was that, so we retired to the Officers Club for a few beers. We'd come a long way since Chapel Hill, we told each other, we'd gotten the breaks and we'd been given the duty we requested. We had no complaints. As to squadron assignments, everybody knew they were drawn from some armchair general's hat — it was the Marine Corps way of spreading its top talent around instead of lumping it all in one unit. Philosophically jollified, we treated the Miramar hills to a chorus of "Katie Malone" walking across the parade ground to the mess hall, and after supper we packed up again to be ready for transportation in the morning.

Marine Corps Air Station El Toro, which sprawls across the orange-grove piedmont west of California's Santa Ana Mountains, was before its closing in 1994 one of the largest military bases in the country, a complex of modern buildings, miles of jet runways and state-of-the-art facilities, but that summer of 1943 it looked like a ramshackle remnant of the barnstorming era — three green wooden barracks, a couple of hangars looming forlornly in clouds of windblown dust, a stilt-legged control tower teetering amid administrative shacks little larger than bungalows. Driving through the main gate, Dege and I took in the whole sorry shebang at a single glance. Our first impressions were not of the spirit-lifting variety.

They began to improve the minute we were dropped off at a headquarters building with a hand-painted legend, VMF 113, on a shingle over the door. Inside, we gave our orders to Squadron Adjutant Percy Smith who riffled through them and looked us over. "Degan and Jones," he grunted. "Good. Glad to have you aboard, we're expecting you. Come in and meet the Skipper."

He ushered us into an adjoining office and placed our orders on a desk behind which sat a stocky shirt-sleeved major with protuberant brown eyes that had a way of burning through your skull all the way down to the soles of your feet. Beneath the wings on his blouse,

"Captain Shirley" (Temple) VMF-113 mascot. MCAS El Toro, 1943.

Pop Flaherty.

slung over the back of a chair, were two rows of campaign ribbons topped by a third row of decorations — Navy Cross, Purple Heart, Presidential Unit Citation with star. He came out from behind his desk and we shook hands with Loren Dale Everton, our new commanding officer.

"Doc" Everton (the nickname derived from his civilian days as a pharmacist in Crofton, Nebraska) was a 28-year-old graduate of his state university, a veteran of the Midway battle and a double-ace with eleven enemy planes to his credit at Guadalcanal. He was a soft-spoken man, unassuming in manner and with a smile at once businesslike and genuinely mirthful. He was pleased to learn we had already checked out in the bent-wing fighter. VMF 113, he told us, was the first squadron to be commissioned at El Toro — that had been on New Years Day, over six months ago, and he was only now filling out its full complement of planes and pilots. Through his office window we could see the flightline with a dozen F4U-1A Corsairs, new models equipped with starboard wing spoilers to help improve the plane's stall characteristics and one-piece bubble canopies instead of the old segmented birdcages.

For his nucleus of senior pilots Doc had coralled three of his former squadron mates of VMF 212, a Guadalcanal fighter unit with a record of 94 aerial victories and two destroyers sunk at a cost of four pilots killed in action — these were Captains Frank "Moon" Drury (Navy Cross), Robert "Pop" Flaherty (DFC) and William "Huckleberry" Watkins (DFC). Among his junior pilots already arrived were several of our flight school buddies, 2nd Lts. Lew Cunningham, "Z.O." Humphreys, Frank Grundler, Joe Chrobuck and Bill Duffy. Straight off, he assigned Dege and me to a six-plane division led by Pop Flaherty and suggested we go without delay to batchelor officers quarters, sign up for a room, move in and unpack, grab some lunch and be ready for an area orientation hop that afternoon. He was expecting more pilots in the next day or two, which would bring his flight roster to full strength. The squadron, he said, was slated to ship out for the Pacific combat area in September, and it was obvious that for Doc Everton every interim day counted; he was going to cram each one as full of tactical training time as we could handle.

Thus began that busy summer, the most remarkable thing about which was how we flight school shavetails were received, actually assimilated, by the Cactus Air Force veterans we'd read so much about at Pensacola. Masters of highly specialized skills, they not only shared their know-how with us aloft but accepted us as companions, co-carousers and friends on the ground. It was a camaraderie we'd not expected, yet it seemed completely natural to them. They were a Brotherhood. The seniors of VMF 114, another squadron forming up across the field, included Robert "Cowboy" Stout, Forbes "Alipang" Bastian and Jack Conger, this last famous for one of the more exuberant victories of the Pacific war — running out of ammunition fighting a Zero over Ironbottom Sound, "Congo" had dispatched his enemy by chewing his rudder off with his propeller. Other Cactus 212 pilots — I remember Captains Bob White, John Massey and Mel Freeman — flew in from time to time to spend a couple of nights drinking in Laguna Beach with their former mates. They all, we knew, had been trained by 212's commander, a Congressional Medal of Honor winner who died in action shortly before 212 was relieved. They revered Col. Harold "Injun Joe" Bauer in ways few are given to revere any man, and they honored his memory by passing what they'd learned from him along to us.

They were a zany bunch, some of them still psychologically strung out from their experiences in the Solomons. One afternoon I heard water running in the head off the readyroom and, it being a strange hour for someone to be taking a bath, I investigated. I found one of these old hands soaping himself in a shower stall, singing and whistling and carrying on, happy as a robin in a spring rain. Seeing me, he shouted, "Hey there, Available, (Doc had nicknamed me after Available Jones, a character in Al Capp's comic strip), come on in, the water's fine. Just getting cleaned up a little, going to ease on into town, big night ahead. See you and the chappies at the Doll's House later, eh?...

I would have thought no more about it had he not been fully clothed, lathering up blouse and trousers of his best green uniform.

One-thirteen was Doc Everton's first command. As in his selection

"Doc"

of flight leaders, he'd put together a Cactus- experienced ordnance department led by Warrant Officer George Garner and Master Sergeant Glenn Sullivan. With all six weapons firing, a Corsair expended 150 rounds of ammunition in a two-second burst and, to drive home his point that the new hit-and-run fighter tactics depended ninety per cent on expert gunnery, he had us out over the ocean shooting up target banners all day and the ordnance crew laboring most of the night to keep our guns in working order.

A gunnery practise hop proceeded as follows. One man would take off towing a 30-foot wire mesh target banner and head out beyond the coast. The rest of the flight would rendezvous with him off San Clemente Island and take up position two or three thousand feet above and ahead of him and a mile or so off to one side. The leader would then make a "high side" pass on the banner, fire a burst and come up to take an identical high-and-ahead position on the opposite side. The rest of the flight would follow in turn. Another type of pass was the "overhead" in which the flight would come in over the banner high and directly above. Firing runs were made by doing a split-S — half-rolling and diving straight down on the target.

Scoring hits in any kind of run depended on estimating a correct lead, which meant aiming precisely far enough in front of the banner so the bullets passed through it instead of ahead or behind. The amount of lead lessened as the angle of attack flattened out from full deflection at an angle of 90 degrees down to 45 and 30 degrees, at which point the attacking plane stopped shooting and dove away. The idea was to decrease lead smoothly throughout the run so the cone of fire remained squarely on the banner. Tracer bullets were interspersed at regular intervals among the armor piercing and incendiary rounds that made up our ammunition belts, and these gave the pilot some indication of where his fire cone was in relation to the target.

At the end of a hop the tow man (flight members took turns "flying tow") would come in over the field and release the banner, which would then be picked up by an ordnance truck and driven to the ready room where individual scores were counted. All bullets were painted, a different color for each plane, and the colored holes were tallied amid much noisy squabbling ("That's a *blue* hole, dummy, what are you, blind?"... "Like hell it is, it's *purple* — it's *mine*!") and individual scores were posted on the readyroom bulletin board. Doc kept a close eye on these, and a great rivalry sprang up for the place of top squadron gun.

I had scored above average in Lee field gunnery training, relaxed exercises compared to our El Toro workouts — it seemed we had time for diversion in those days, and some very odd things happened. I remember the morning one of our flight- happy Lee mechanics, tantalized beyond endurance by watching us land and take off in our Grummans day after day, suddenly jumped into the Piper Cub that served the field as a wind indicator, started the engine and jockeyed it off the ground into the air. We stood watching in amazement while he flew dips and dives and wobbly gyrations around the field, then tried to get it back down before it ran out of gas. He lost his nerve, gunned it around in a circle and tried once more. He did this several times before he finally chopped the throttle at twenty feet above the runway, flopped down in a semi-stall and brought the Cub to a stop just short of the field perimeter fence. He stepped out of it with a happy grin on his face and we cheered him mightily as he was led off by security guards.

In our El Toro gunnery drills I continued to stay well up in the scoring. At first I attributed this to the luck of having been blessed from birth with exceptional distance vision. Also, I felt comfortable in the new "One-Able" F4U; its seat was higher in the cockpit than the birdcage model and its bubble canopy made for vastly improved visibility. As time went on, though, I began thinking about something my instructor told me back in elementary flight training. He was fanatical about smoothness at the controls, coordinating aileron, rudder and elevator movements to eliminate skidding or jerkiness in the flight path. I asked him why all the emphasis on smoothness. He replied, "It's not to fly pretty, it's to fly *good.*"

I pondered this, seeking applications in other areas. I thought of Fred Astair doing a soft-shoe routine, of Sam Snead driving a golf ball a quarter of a mile, of Joe DiMaggio stroking a baseball into the center field bleachers. I thought of my days in eight-oared racing shells, how it had occurred to me early that whereas a smoothly coordinated rowing form looks pretty its real importance is that it applies maximum body power to move the boat. In every case it made sense: *good* came first — the smoother the use of the power available the better the performance, and *pretty* followed automatically.

So from my first days in yellow peril biplanes I had made myself a slave to the needle-ball indicator in the instrument panel. Keeping needle and ball centered during a maneuver assured a neat balance of control surfaces and the cleanest possible cleavage through the air, and this, having become so natural that I no longer needed to look at the indicator, had to be paying off while both eyes were glued to the Mark 8 reflector gunsight and all concentration was on estimating target lead and squeezing off a burst at exactly the right second.

Pay off it did; one afternoon I put 33 per cent of my expended ammunition through the banner to make top gun on the bulletin board and earn the honor of picking up the beer tab in the Officers Club that evening.

The summer wore on, gruelling, exhilarating weeks in which we followed a day's flying with a hot shower, a change into clean khakis and a happy hour before supper. Major Everton, puffing a cigar, tossed back an occasional preprandial bourbon with us. Doc had a tremendous feeling for "his boys", a feeling that was reciprocated in ever increasing measure as time went by. We noticed that in the eyes of his old 212 comrades he was someone special, and in his quiet way he met us tyros on our own terms, giving us the sense that he knew and cared about us personally. He also ran a taut ship. He got rid of anyone he considered less than top pilot material, starting with those who looked like they might kill themselves or somebody else. A few tried. One new man locked on a target banner in an overhead pass, smashed his propeller flying through it and parachuted into Catalina Channel. He was fished out unharmed by a Navy tug, but the next day his locker was empty and he was seen no more. Another newcomer bounced on landing, slammed on his brakes, flipped his plane onto its back and cut his hand off between the windscreen and the runway.

Inevitably, even good pilots had bad moments, off-center reactions or reflexes that resulted in crack-ups. One morning in August Bill Duffy somersaulted on landing, ruptured a fuel tank and caught fire. Sgt. Glenn Sullivan, nearby with his ordnance crew, scrambled under the wreckage to get him out of the cockpit but couldn't reach him, whereupon Major Charlie Kimak, our executive officer who was smaller than Sully, wriggled under, released his safety belt and pulled him clear of the flames. His flight suit was burned to a crisp and his body scorched head-to-toe by third degree burns. We went to see him in sickbay but he was delerious and didn't recognize us.

Duff's accident occurred the day before I had a visit from my older brother, a Navy ensign undergoing armed guard training in San Diego. Seaver had just learned that his wife had delivered their first child, a girl they'd named Jan Andrea for Louise's mother and me. He also brought news of our sister in the Red Cross. Sis had sent me one of her little red and white enamel collar devices which I had pinned on my flying helmet for luck, and Seaver told me she was presently at sea, headed for hospital duty somewhere in the Pacific. We had a celebrational evening on the town and the next morning I took him up in an SNJ for a ride, concluding it with a couple of linked slow rolls and a three-turn spin to relax his nerves. He was a good sport; back on the ground he told Doc and the others that it was very exciting and great fun, but if he had to fight a war he preferred to do it on the deck of a merchant ship with his gun crew.

That afternoon I drove him to the bus station in Laguna. Returning to the field I learned that Duff had died a half hour before. Lew Cunningham took his body back to his family in Boston. For me it was a sobering trade-off: a namesake niece gained and a good friend gone forever.

In the first week of September Pop Flaherty married Jeannie Cabane of Emerald Bay whom he'd been courting all summer. He insisted that the five of us in his training flight participate in his nuptials; he picked Dege to be best man because he knew the Catholic marriage procedure, he laid usher duty on Z.O., Lew and John

Author's brother, Seaver Jones, at Armed Guard School, San Diego, CA, fall of 1943.

Fitting and he asked me to sing Gounod's *Ave Maria* from the organ loft because he considered my singing voice the least objectionable in the group. The ceremony went smoothly and he and Jeannie took off for a honeymoon at Lake Tahoe.

Pop's timing was unfortunate, however, because he missed our first full-squadron cross-country hop. We'd already been issued Colt .45 automatics in shoulder holsters and the Skipper's announcement of this flight was further evidence that our departure for destinations unknown was drawing nigh. His pre-hop briefing was characteristically to the point. Since Guadalcanal, he told us, the nature of fighter squadron missions had changed from defensive to offense; instead of hanging onto a beleagured island with teeth and toenails, scrambling aircraft pellmell to intercept incoming hostile bombers and their escorting zeros, we were now taking the war to the enemy, moving up through the Bismarck Archipelago toward the Central Pacific islands and the Philippines. Long distance flights over water were involved, fuel consumption would be a problem and formation flexibility would be the watchword. The two-plane section, a leader and his wingman, was still the lowest common fighting denominator and the four-plane division, consisting of two sections, remained the basic tactical unit. A squadron strike would be made up of several divisions with his own at the head of the formation, and that was how we would fly to the Arizona border and back. To simulate a live target approach we would observe radio silence.

We took off on a cloudless mid-afternoon, joined up in a climb headed east across the Santa Anas toward the desert and levelled of in smooth-as-silk air at angels ten. What struck us immediately was the silence in our headphones. A training flight with its violent maneuvering and racing around the sky involved a lot of radio chatter but now, cruising in procession with only the drone of engines in our ears, we were transported by the spectacle of our aircraft tucked together in four-plane clusters, wingtips almost touching, dipping a foot or two here and there, easing back into position.

Half an hour passed in straight and level flight before we swung around the Salton Sea and headed back to the coast. The sun rested low on the edge of a milky desert haze, we kept our eyes on Doc's lead plane. Every so often I glanced out to port where Z.O. hung motionless a little below and behind my left aileron grinning like a gargoyle.

With the mountains in sight Doc began to descend and signalled everyone to drop into line-of-divisions astern. That done, each division eased into step-down right echelon. Minutes later we swarmed in over the field and began the break- up ballet, snapping off at 10-second intervals, dropping wheels and flaps and swinging onto base leg. On the tar after the landing strip run-out we gunned around and taxied back to the flightline, blowing huge clouds of dust across the field with our propwash. Minutes later, walking from the line to the readyroom with chutes over our shoulders, somebody started to sing:

I saw a lady yesterday
Knitting three socks of blue,
I stopped and asked the lady why
She did not knit but two,
She said she had heard from her son
Who in his letter put
That since he'd joined the Army
He had grown another foot. . .
We felt good, we felt pretty - we felt ready.

One night during the following week our planes disappeared from the flightline. A hush descended on the base. Nobody knew anything. When queried, the Skipper said all he'd received was an order from group headquarters saying absolute security was to be maintained concerning the absence of our aircraft — there was to be no talk about it on or off the station, we were to go about our business and carry on as usual.

These instructions were clearly not being observed in Laguna Beach; when a group of us arrived that night and began carrying on as usual we were greeted with sly winks and knowing smiles. Fred, the bartender at the Doll's House, told us to put back our wallets and said, "For you guys, everything's on the house." It was the same all over town — our money was no good anywhere. At one point as we were strolling in full-throated song down Coast Boulevard, the front door of a house flung wide and a woman rushed out and shrieked, "You boys are comin' inside! You don't go out to fight them goddam Japs without havin' a drink with us!" She hustled us into a noisy ruckus of bedragled Hollywood types — an English character actor with false teeth, a retired wardrobe mistress, her husband, others, everyone sloshed, people climbing in and out of windows, voices coming from under the sofa. After swigging scoops of gin and grapefruit juice from a bowl the size of a bathtub we thanked them all and squirmed our way outside to freedom. So much for absolute security orders at El Toro.

The next day word was passed: all squadron personnel restricted to base, pack your gear, be prepared to board busses in front of the BOQ at 0500 tomorrow. Frank Drury flew an SNJ up to Lake Tahoe and buzzed Pop's honeymoon hideaway, signalling him to return home pronto. We loafed around through the day, turned in early, and as the sun crested the mountains next morning we started rolling south through orange groves along the California coast. In San Diego we were ferried across the bay to the naval base on North Island. There moored alongside the main dock lay the biggest ship any of us had ever seen, it was *Bunker Hill*, one the the new *Essex*-class "fast carriers" about to begin her maiden shakedown cruise in the Pacific. Her flight deck, four stories above our heads, was crammed solidly with lashed-down, wing-folded Corsairs.

Not all were ours as we learned in the next minute when Curly Lehnert and Chick Whalen emerged from the dockside crowd to grab Dege and me — VMF 422 had arrived from Santa Barbara the day before and would be shipping out with us. They'd spent the night on board and, learning 113 was coming from El Toro, had saved us a couple of bunks in the ship's low-rent district reserved for transient officers. What information did they have that we didn't — would we be flying off this wagon? No, we're going along as passengers. Going where? Unspecified; sailing orders were sealed. By the time we'd stowed our gear and caught up a bit after three months separation it was almost noon.

We went up to the flight deck to make sure our planes were properly secured and have a look around. From the edge of the deck we looked down on the madhouse along the wharf, acres of snorting, yelling, clanging activity, sailors in blue workshirts and greasy white caps swarming in and out of the ship, flatulent trucks, scuttling fork lifts and front-end loaders packing last minute stores and equipment aboard. At the foot of the gangway we noticed Major Everton conferring with a group of our noncoms. (Sgt. Sullivan, we learned later, was suffering an attack of 'Canal-contracted malaria; he was running a 104 temperature and having trouble coordinating. Doc spotted the problem and asked him if he wanted help. He shook his head, fearing the Navy would take notice and keep him ashore. Doc told him to go on up the gangplank. He followed his ordnance chief aboard, got him bedded down out of the way and that night, with the ship well out to sea, took him to sickbay for treatment.)

Standing apart from this group was another, our married pilots solemnly holding hands with their wives — Joe Chrobuck and Babe, Z.O. and Betty Jean (pregnant), Pop and Dick Potter with their brides.

Eyeing this glum assemblage, Dege shook his head. "I've got nothing against women," he muttered, "but right now I'm glad I'm single."

By late afternoon dock hustle was tapering off and stowage compartments were slamming shut all over the ship. Brass was in evidence on the bridge now, a ramrod-straight admiral staring seaward with hands clasped behind his rump, ship's officers pacing the catwalk and glancing at their wrist watches. Not wanting to miss departure activities we hurried through supper in the transient officers mess, a refectory vaguely reminiscent of a Vermont farmer's milking shed, and were back on the flight deck as turbines began rumbling deep in *Bunker*'s bowels. Navy tugs waited alongside the carrier's hull, the dock was deserted except for sailors standing by hausers fore and aft.

Suddenly the North Island station band marched out of the administration building and, taking position at dock-center, struck up "Anchors Aweigh". Bells clanged on the bridge, boatswains shouted orders on the wharf, lines were cast off and the tugs began nudging the largest warship in the U.S. Navy out into the Coronado roadstead.

We'd seen the sun rise that morning, and half an hour later as we sat along the edge of the flight deck we watched it slide beneath the horizon directly ahead of us. The tugs dropped their lines and turned back toward the darkening California coastline. We hummed along, cleaving gentle Pacific swells under ship's power while the white eye of Point Loma light drifted by to the north. Two blacked-out destroyers appeared out of nowhere and took up escort positions a mile or so off our bows. . .

The moment remains a vision in memory. We sit quietly as darkness deepens, our feet dangling in the safety nets. No one speaks. The sea surging beneath us works a spell as the ship heaves along in its majestic westering. An Aldis lamp blinks Morse code from a destroyer bridge far across the water. For a long time we sit absorbed in private thoughts. There is no need for talk and there is, in fact, only one thought which we share individually, each in his own fashion. It is simple, profound, astonishing: the moment we've looked forward to for eighteen months has arrived, it's here; we don't know where we're going or what's in store for us or how we'll handle it when it comes, but we don't have to worry about these things right now — not yet. It's enough to realize that after all this time of preparation we're actually on our way to apply what we've learned in mortal earnest. . .

Chapter Three

During World War II much meretricious drivel was written about our new fast attack carriers which started coming on line in mid-1943 (*Essex* was the first, in May). Experts of every persuasion declared them economically unsound and too easy to sink, old salt correspondents from America's cornbelt compared them to their sleek escorting cruisers and destroyers and laid on them such epithets as clumsy, cowshaped, lopsided, topheavy. It made for attention-grabbing copy, perhaps, but any ignorant Oahu farmer who looked up from his taro patch to behold Bunker Hill standing off Diamond Head the morning of October 2, 1943, would have had less jaded and far truer impressions. Observed from a distance in a luminescent dawn mist she was, first of all, *big* — spectral, monstrous, a ghost-gray apparition, something like a recumbent Empire State Building plowing through the ocean. From any angle, under any conditions, she looked formidable, awesome, threatful; but, always and mostly, just plain BIG.

In our four days and nights aboard we had fallen in with her rhythms, watch changes, mess sittings, flight operations, the spotting and respotting of her 70-odd aircraft. That morning off Hawaii Frank Grundler and I stood on the forward flight deck watching pretty little silver flying fish skitter out ahead of her bow wave, flit over glassy swells for fifty feet or so before plopping back into the water. Our mood was pensive and, as far as the ship was concerned, respectful; a brief taste of sea duty had expanded our land-oriented notions of military aviation, and though we knew more of these 27,000- ton floating cities were under construction at shipyards back home we never imagined that by 1945 we would have as many as seventeen in action. They were the enemy's top-priority targets and they took heavy battle damage from conventional air and *kamikaze* attacks (*Bunker* had her forward end blown off at Okinawa) but not one of them went to the bottom. Moreover, those who judged them clumsy and vulnerable had to eat their words at war's end when American fast carriers, submarines and B-29 Superforts were given the lion's share of credit in destroying Japan's war-making capability. Consensus among historians on such a point would never be achieved but many of them on both sides of the conflict agreed that our atomic bombs merely capped what our big ships and aircraft had already accomplished.

On that San Diego-Hawaii passage *Bunker* was piggy-backing the Corsairs of three squadrons on her flight deck — ours and those of 422 and VF-17, the last being one of only two Navy Corsair squadrons existing at the time. Led by Lt. Cdr. John Thomas "Tommy" Blackburn, VF-17 would shortly begin a distinguished career in the South Pacific, but its pilots had been delt a grave disappointment while aboard; they'd expected to operate off *Bunker* as part of her air group, only to learn when their orders were finally opened that they'd be replaced in Pearl Harbor by a squadron of Grumman F6Fs, fighter planes considered more suitable for carrier ops than the temperamental and still relatively untried F4U. They'd be put ashore in Pearl with us Marines.

We were disappointed too for we hoped we'd be taken down south and let off somewhere in the war zone instead of being dumped at Oahu. But, once again, orders were orders, and the Skipper seemed happy with them. We could use more air time, he told us. We'd be stationed at MCAS Ewa (pronounced Ev-ah) on Barbers Point where we'd participate in "war exercises". We'd be going south soon enough, he said.

Nudging slowly into the Pearl approaches in mid-morning we could see evidence of the Jap attack two years before — bits of skeletonized superstructure poking above the water along battleship row, remnants of demolished buildings and heavy equipment strewn around miles of shoreline. We eased into the channel, closer to the wreckage, and the full impact of what had happened here hit us while *Bunker* was mooring at Ford Island; it was the appalling realization — not an idea any more but a confrontational fact — that a whole nation of people can be led by power-mad maniacs into taking another by surprise and destroying it on the largest possible scale. We had stepped into the actuality of war, *world* war. And in that moment we knew also that we'd better get used to it.

An hour later we were loaded on busses and driven around Honolulu, through miles of sisal barrens and into more unhappy history. We'd been briefed concerning the debacle here at our destination. At five minutes before eight o'clock on that Sunday morning in '41 a flight of Zeroes, 21 of them in the van of the attack, had come swarming down over the mountains and within half an hour had all but blown the small Marine air station near the village of Ewa off the map. Resistance was catch-as-catch-can; lacking anti-aircraft weapons, defenders of Air Group 21 fought Zeros and Val dive bombers with pistols and rifles. Two men jumped into a parked SBD and shot a Val down with its rear seat machine gun, but when the rest started back to their carriers they left the station in flames, one of the men in the SBD mortally wounded, and all of the 47 aircraft sitting on the flightline destroyed.

In following weeks MCAS Ewa was restored to fighting condition. New buildings were constructed, its single runway extended and another added. Marine Air Group 23 was formed in March to undertake regular sea patrols and conduct defensive operations if the Japs came back. They didn't, and by the time we arrived, seventeen months after the decisive battle of Midway, the station was a staging base for squadrons on their way to combat.

In matters of comeliness Ewa was a big step up from El Toro, as were its dust-free climate and general living conditions. We were housed in one-floor, wood-and-screen barracks garlanded with bouganvillea and surrounded by flower beds. Wild orchids hung in trees, island doves cooed in the shrubbery, tropical flora grew everywhere in profusion. We messed on island beef and fresh produce in a dining hall modelled on a Samoan *fale* and we watched the latest movies twice a week under star-studded skies. We were in Dorothy Lamour la-la land, complete with giggling *wahines* to make up our bunks and sweep the floors, and while we itched to go south into action (VF-17 had gone on ahead of us) we knew we were a lot more comfortable than we would be when we got there.

Our flying duty at Ewa was, actually, very close to the real thing. The war exercises Doc had mentioned had two purposes: to test Oahu's radar defense network (a matter of some concern after its fluky performance in '41) and to provide the island's resident and transient fighter squadrons with realistic combat situations. These were reenactments of the Pearl Harbor fiasco, pitting Navy and Marine attackers against Army defenders. The day before the exercise, attacking units deployed to the outer islands of Maui, Kauai and Hawaii from which, at dawn next day, they came in at random altitudes and directions. The idea was for Radar Command to pick them up on its scopes, sort out individual elements and scramble the three Army P-47 squadrons

A two-plane section, leader and wingman. (Courtesy of the National Archives.)

based at Stanley Field to intercept them before they could reach the harbor.

The idea was sound and the exercises were great training. I recall our first in which Doc led us into the target area flat out at wavetop level, a thousand feet below the P-47s snarling around in the clouds looking for us. We swarmed in over Hickam Field taking wing camera photographs of parked B- 17s and transport aircraft which, had we been using our guns, we would have blasted to rubble. The P-47s found us at last and chased us into the hills where we turned to engage them, going around and around at heavy Gs, graying out, pulling tiny corkscrew contrails off our wingtips until we were taking more pictures of our gunsight pips centered on their rudders. The Army fighter jocks were good — they were taking pictures of us, too — and we all ended up in one glorious roaring whirligig brawl over the city of Honolulu that sent its citizens scuttling for cover and writing nasty letters to the newspapers.

Ewa was easy living and exhilarating duty but we continued to badger Doc to get us out of this wing camera nonsense and into some real shooting. He smiled at our impatience and recounted a parable his old commander, Col. Bauer, used to tell the eager young pilots of VMF 212 while they were training at Efate to go into action at the 'Canal. "There were these two bulls standing on a hill looking down at a meadow full of cows," Doc would drawl with his deadpan humor and puffing on his cigar. "The young bull says to the old bull, come on, Dad, let's run down there and knock a couple of 'em off. The old bull paws the ground, looks at the youngster and says, I've got a better idea, Son; let's *walk* down there and knock 'em *all* off. . ."

In the middle of our two months on Oahu, VMF-225 arrived with more of our old flight school buddies, among them my St. Paul's School and Princeton classmates Hunter Gcaig and Jack Butler. John Crosby Butler, Jr., who had also been with me at St. Paul's School, was the only son of a gracious Virginia lady and a country squire he referred to as "the Colonel". A lithe-of-build sportsman, Jack was handsome in the Arrow Collar Man tradition and deadly on nubile females which he stalked with Groucho Marx-style intensity. Actually he didn't have to work all that hard for they seemed unable to resist him — over the years I watched more than one who, upon meeting him for the first time and ex-

Jack Butler.

changing ten minutes of fidgety babble, suddenly rolled her eyes heavenward and glomed onto him like a love-struck abalone. Jack drank Old Bushmills Irish Whiskey, and while thus engaged at the O-club bar the afternoon before Thanksgiving he reminded me that we had another SPS classmate, Henry Alexander Walker, who lived on Nuuanu Avenue in town. I suggested we call "Ali Pineapple" and wish him a pleasant holiday. Ali told us that his family had a party in progress and insisted that we come join it, so we purloined a jeep in the O-club parking lot and started for the city.

It was a wild ride. At one point we missed a turn in the road and went flying off into a cane field where we bounced and thrashed and stopped in a spine-shattering stall. "A.B.," gentleman farmer Butler said after a moment, "you know what a jeep has in common with a stud boar's reproductive organ?" I shook my head. "They're both comfortable *in a pig's ass.*"

The Walker mansion driveway was lined with black limousines bearing gold-starred license plates. Jack registered dismay at so much Navy brass on the premises. "Listen, buster," I said, parking our battered old jeep at the head of the line, "we are travelling Marines and we'll not be deterred by a gaggle of local swabjockies. Agreed?" He nodded. "Okay, follow me."

Ali met us in the hall, put flagons of Thanksgiving cheer in our hands and introduced us, his two khaki-clad 2nd lieutenant schoolmates, to several braided and dress-uniformed guests, also to his younger sister Ann who immediately took Butler in tow. There was a poker game going in the library, Ali said to me, and a seat open if I was interested. I was, and in the next breath I found myself sitting at a table in a dark, book-lined room facing a circle of very senior officers with gold shoulder boards and fruit salad all over their chests. Hearing Jack, Ali and Ann chortling behind my chair, I peeked over my cards to study my opponents more carefully. . .

A white-haired, pappy-looking gent with squinty blue eyes at the head of the table — God's teeth, I gasped to myself, *it's Admiral Nimitz!*

. . .A thin-faced, solemn looking personage directly across — *Admiral Spruance!*

. . .To my right, a hefty type, built like a fire hydrant — *Admiral Fletcher!*

Obviously in on the joke, they were all smiling benignly at the newcomer to their midst. I put down my cards, swallowing hard. Something was expected of me. What? What to say? Well, what else? I pushed back my chair and hollered, "*Who's minding the store?*"

The evening went well after that (I even got up nerve enough to raise the Commander in Chief, Pacific, on paired queens and nines) and Jack and I made it back to Ewa at two in the morning.

Increasingly restless as the weeks went by, we flew more Pearl Harbor exercises and, on off hours, organized inter-department football games and swimming trips to Kanakalua Point for the men. Several of us celebrated making 1st lieutenant by throwing a luau for our fellows. We saw Ali occasionally; when he was running low on gas he drove out to the field where Jack and I saved him ration stamps by filling his 1936 Ford with 100-octane aviation fuel, cutting each tankful of the powerful stuff with kerosene. These inroads into the tax-payers' gasoline supply were reported by our weekly squadron newspaper, THE U-MAN COMEDY, which was edited by Lt. Russ Drumm and written by a young corporal from the New York suburbs named Art Buchwald. "Little Artie", as he was known, was the Sad Sack of the Boom Room (ordnance department), the butt of his own journalistic jokes. "We had to teach him to drive a truck," his chief, Sgt. Sullivan, says today of America's favorite newspaper humorist. "He didn't know *anything*!" He laughs. "But, boy, look

Bill Degan.

Maj. Everton and Capt. Vic Erickson, Engebi, 1944.

at him now!"

Our impatience to get on with the war reached its peak when we learned that our Bunker Hill shipmates of VF-17 had on their first encounter with enemy aircraft splashed five Zeros off Cape Torokina in the northern Solomons. It was almost too much to bear. Bill Degan expressed his frustration that night when an officer of Ewa's permanent staff began heckling one of our pilots, Capt. Victor Erickson. Bill listened for awhile, the back of his neck slowly turning pink. With his long hook nose (we called him "Hawk"), massive bow legs and shoulders, Bill Degan could terrorize whole neighborhoods simply by walking through them and glowering at the citizenry. He listened to the officer's taunting as long as he could, then he said to Vic, "Captain, do you like the Dege?" Vic, knowing Degan and his ways, saw what was coming. He grinned. "Yes, lieutenant," he said, "I like the Dege." Degan turned slowly to his tormenter and hit him so hard his feet left the ground and he sprawled full length on his back, out like a light. Dege then plucked a couple of blooms from a nearby Oleander bush and laid them gently on the sleeping giant's chest. "*Requiescat in Pacem*," he said, and walked away.

Finally, in the week between Christmas and New Years, we had one of those tips by which the Skipper told us our long- awaited departure was imminent — he announced that anyone who so desired could buy a case of out-of-bond whiskey from the station's stores, adding with a wry smile that these supplies would follow us wherever we went in future. Two nights later he called all his officers, air and ground, together and read our orders. We were to leave in two contingents: our total complement of twenty-four planes and as many pilots would go by aircraft carrier, the rest of the pilots and the 260-odd officers and men of the ground detachment were to come later by troop transport. Again, our destination would not be made known until we were at sea.

Next morning we of the flight echelon were roused before daylight. Those of the ground detachment got up to join us for our last breakfast at Ewa and see us on our way to the carrier waiting at Ford Island. It was a small one, the escort carrier *White Plains* — our wing-folded Corsairs lashed down topside took up most of its flight deck — and our departure was low-key, even hush-hush, no bands, bells or whistles this time; the ship simply tossed away her mooring lines and eased out into the channel.

The sun was well up by the time we took position at the center of a convoy of supply ships and transports off Diamond Head. Flanked by a protective cordon of destroyers, all vessels bent on speed and turned their bows seaward. Hours later, after the Hawaian Islands had dropped below the northern horizon, the bullhorn on the bridge announced that we were headed for one of the lesser of the Gilbert Islands, a speck in the ocean 2000 miles away called Tarawa.

The battle for the three-mile coral island of Betio, code named "Helen", in the Tarawa atoll had been one of the bloodiest in Marine Corps history. Six weeks before, infantry assault waves of the 2nd Division had stranded their LCVPs in shoal waters of the lagoon and been forced to wade ashore hundreds of yards through murderous artillery crossfire from the beach. Enormous casualties had been incurred and the information we received was that mopping up had yet to be completed; as *White Plains* churned southward we were told that snipers on the island's east end were still being shot out of trees and rooted out of tunnels.

Rumors pertaining to the Tarawa campaign were being handed around the ship like candy bars ("Hey, didja hear that. . .", "Yeah, but lissen, I just heard . . .") and one concerning how the number of soldiers on Helen had been estimated before the attack was intriguing enough to run down. I traced it to a ninety-day-wonder ensign who had started out in Naval Intelligence and still had connections there. He looked like an intelligence type — hair hanging over his collar, twitchy hands, darty eyes. "Quite simple," he said with a clever shrug. "ONI had a copy of Japanese army regulations, very specific on latrine facilities in the field, how the sheds were to be built and, notably, the number of holes in each — there had to be one hole for every fifteen men in the garrison. Japs always go strictly by the book, you know. At Tarawa they built their latrines over the lagoon, right out in plain sight. . . " He looked at me expectantly. "See how it was done?"

"Not yet."

"Aerial photographs!" he exclaimed, exasperated at my stupidity. "Take pictures, measure the length of the latrine sheds, figure the average width of a Jap soldier's rear end, do a little arithmetic. Simple as that."

"How did the estimate check out?" I asked.

"Check out?"

"Sure — count the dead, count prisoners taken, do a little arithmetic. Simple as that."

He shrugged again and turned away. "Haven't heard the results," he muttered over his shoulder.

I laughed. The story was just crazy enough to be credible and I determined to verify it if I could (I didn't: I heard more versions of it, some that even had the arithmetical estimate right on the money, but they never got beyond the Hey-didja-hear level).

I spent many shipboard hours in the metal shop making a grip for a knife blade a SeaBee blacksmith at Ewa had fashioned for me. He'd examined my standard issue survival knife and offered to make me a better one. He did so by shaping and forging a length of jeep-spring steel, a marvellous job of old fashioned hammer-and-anvil craftsmanship — it was 18-inches long and weighed about three pounds with a tang threaded at the end to receive a threaded aluminum knob. I made a hand guard for it from a piece of forged aluminum and modelled the grip by laminating alternate thicknesses of sheet aluminum and hard rubber matting, drilling a hole lengthwise through them and sliding them onto the tang shishkabob-style. The end knob was then screwed on and a securing bolt drilled through it. I'm not handy at homecraft benchwork, and when I'd ground the grip assembly into shape and felt the swing and balance of the completed machete-knife I was very proud of myself.

Its size was a problem, though, for our combat survival gear was extensive and bulky. Over baggy one-piece flight suits we wore a Mae West flotation jacket, oxygen mask, Colt .45 sidearm, dye marker and shark repellent packets, fishing kit, hand flares, signalling mirror, life raft and parachute. We also wore a web belt with a canteen of fresh water. I decided to carry the machete on my belt and made a rivetted leather sheath that slung it at my hip beneath my parachute harness. It was an uncomfortable arrangement, something like the boot camp recruit's ordeal of sleeping with his rifle, but it worked well enough.

The weather held fair all the way down to the sixth parallel two hundred miles north of our launch point. During lunch our last day aboard we were startled by an astonishing sound, a prolonged agonized squeal emanating from a portable radio we had tuned to a Stateside radio station. Buried within the static and caterwauling a male voice was crooning "Don't Sit Under the Apple Tree with Anyone Else but Me-e-e-e." We stared at each other. What the hell is this? The announcer filled us in — it was a stage appearance by a new singer, a skinny kid with jug ears and a protuberant Adam's apple. Frank Sinatra was creating a sensation among the bobbysoxers back home and the squealing was their collective expression of the mating urge.

White Plains' flight deck was too short to permit normal carrier take-off so that afternoon her air officer gave us an on-deck lecture/demonstration on the niceties of a front end launching by catapult. None of us had been shot into the sky off a ship's bow before, and whereas it seemed a

Doc Everton stenciled his wife's maiden name on the cowling.

simple operation (hold your head back against the pad, close your eyes and think of something else), anything that new and spectacular in flying procedures, especially upon entering a war zone, was bound to raise anxiety levels. Mine was eased somewhat when, in the middle of the talk, I suddenly thought of a name for my plane, #55. Like the bomber boys in Europe we'd been stencilling names on our Corsair cowlings. Doc had christened his (#44) "Dolores Barrett" after his wife, Dege called his (#36) "The Fighting Irishman", Lew adapted his street address in Lincoln, Mass., "Tower Road Terror." Now I hit on one I considered worthy of my own trusty, much-loved U-bird; from that point on, southbound by slingshot at latitude 6 degrees north, Corsair #55 of VMF-113 would be known as "The Sudden Jerk".

At 0600 next morning we were rousted out of our bunks and told to report on the double for chow, a quick Australian-style breakfast of steak and eggs, after which we gathered in the ready room and began draping on flight gear. We were issued metal helmets and trenching tools while an officer of the convoy commander's staff briefed us on meteorological conditions. He described the airfield on Helen. "Land short," he said. "Park alongside the strip, get out of your aircraft, dig yourself a hole, get in it and stay there until sniper fire, if any, is suppressed and the gas truck arrives. . ."

We had a long flight ahead of us that day. After topping off gas tanks on Helen we would depart for Apamama, another of the Gilberts further south; there we'd refuel again and proceed to Funafuti in the Ellice Islands below the equator — a total of 700 over-water miles. We would receive our next orders on Funafuti, the officer said in closing. Were there any questions? Somebody asked about the radio range on Tarawa. His answer was not reassuring. "If it's working it'll get you close aboard," he said. "After that — well, don't worry, you'll smell the island before you see it. If you get lost just crack your cockpit canopy and follow your nose. Good luck. . ." He nodded to the watch officer, a button was pushed somewhere and the ready room squawk box bawled, "Pilots, man your planes."

Trotting with our chutes, shovels and potty helmets along the ill-lit passageway, we were thrown off balance as the ship began her ponderous swing into the wind; we bounced off bulkheads, stumbled between blackout curtains, through the hatch and out onto the flight deck where we found there was no wind, only a faint breeze riffling an oily-calm, mist-shrouded sea — *White Plains* was charging ahead at flank speed to produce maximum airflow over the deck for the launchings. The scene was not reassuring — half an hour after sunrise the sky was obscured by a milky overcast, plane handlers and catapult crewmen in brightly colored coveralls were moving listlessly about among our aircraft, waiting for us. We paused, standing together in a group silently taking it all in; then we slapped shoulders, grunted parting words and hurried off, each man to his plane.

There followed for me an unsettling moment which I suspect many single-seat fighter pilots, however eager, knew while climbing up on the wing, clambering into the cockpit and strapping themselves in. Back at Pensacola Dege, Chick and I had chosen to fly fighters for reasons we discussed together, but I had another I'd kept to myself: I didn't want to be responsible for the life of a man in a rear seat; I wanted to know that, whatever I did in the air, only I would suffer the consequences. Taken at the philosophical level I'd elected for lone-eagle solitude, and while we were forming the squadron at El Toro I learned I had a price to pay for it; I found that the process of going down the check-off list and starting my engine was always accompanied by an inexplicable feeling of isolation. I would look along the flightline at my fellows, all busy with the same chores I was — they were right there, we'd been together on the ground a minute before and we'd be together in the sky very shortly, but during this pre-flight heads-down absorption inside our mechanical cocoons there seemed to exist a void between us, a separateness that was more than physical.

It loomed large that gloomy morning with my cockpit open to the damp sea air, engines thundering on every hand and implike figures, suddenly come alive, darting around directing planes toward the launch position. Trying to concentrate on my instruments, I took the moment for a revelation of truth, a glimpse of our mortal accountability: we arrive in the world alone, I thought, we depart it alone, and, even if we know friendship, loyalty and, hopefully, love in the interim, I'm probably getting in this bleak moment as true a picture of the human condition as I will ever have.

In the months and years ahead I would come to learn better than this.

Our Corsairs had been spotted in order of take-off and Pop Flaherty was already taxiing into position in front of me. Tongues of orange flame flickered from his engine exhaust ports as he revved up and squared away. The sea mist was burning off, I could make out the dark shapes of convoy vessels around the horizon standing by while the carrier discharged its cargo. . .

In the next instant a blast of steam exploded under my nose and Pop shot away like a giant bat, dipped slightly toward the water then zoomed up and off into the gloaming, chasing after Doc's division ahead. . .

The action runs together at this point. The spotter imps, their arms whirling frantically, motioned me forward; I eased on power, crept slowly to the launch line, set flaps and held position with full brakes while the catapult was hooked up. Then I shoved the throttle forward to the stop and gave the launch officer a thumbs up, at which he dropped his wand and a force like a 60 mph rear end highway collision flung me off the bow. All I remember of the seconds after the jolt was gingerly adjusting trim tabs while the gray-black sea dropped away below. Then suddenly, in recollection, everything becomes routine — retract wheels, close canopy, reduce power. Light strengthens, visibility increases as the Jerk gains altitude and the morning sun pokes over the mist to reveal Doc's division several miles ahead. I see Pop trailing it, turning for me to cut inside him and join up. Now Dege is coming along right behind me, rising above the overcast. My spirit, literally winged, soars with an elation no earthling will ever know. I'm in the air again, I'm back with the fellows once more, all is well. . .

Part Two
Razor Base

Chapter Four

The smell was not so bad, nothing to what we'd soon encounter in the Marshalls where the dead were still above ground, but the visual impression of that war-trashed tropical islet called Helen was stunningly, dumfoundingly out of this world — I mean *literally* out, a meteor-blasted planetscape, a vista of churned, jagged coral with fire-blackened tree trunks strewn around like kindling on the far side of Pluto. Here and there groups of helmeted Marines, weapons at the ready, poked about in the rubble or stood talking in hushed voices, staring at each other as though they couldn't believe what they'd done or even that it had happened at all. But it had happened, and they'd done it. The Japs had tunnelled Tarawa like a giant cheese and fought for it from underground bunkers so thickly overlaid with cocoanut logs that they'd held up under air strikes, naval bombardment and conventional infantry tactics — after desperate inch-by-inch rifle and flamethrower assault these same combat-exhausted zombies had finally knocked them out by bulldozing tons of loose coral up against the gunports, pouring gasoline down the air vents and immolating the occupants.

By the time we landed that morning the island had been secured and most of the snipers rooted out of their tunnels. The sun burned relentlessly in the sky, over the lagoon there hung a ghastly silence. Out there hundreds had died wading in to the beach, hundreds more had been killed hunkering for protection against the sea wall close to where I was standing - - this ravaged Helen had launched more ships and created more carnage than Homer ever dreamed in his wildest nightmares. Beyond the outer reef the sea shimmered in a freshening breeze but here over the atoll there clung a steamy, suffocating stillness. Staring around with sweat stinging my eyes I could feel only a cowardly kind of gratitude that I would be flying my airborne foxhole high above whatever Tarawas lay waiting for us in the months ahead.

While the gas truck was making its way up the line a weary-eyed noncom wandered over and walked around the Jerk, studying it from every angle. His helmet and cammo suit were caked with grime, also with a crusty reddish substance that could be but one thing (and it wasn't his). He swung his carbine in one hand shillelagh-fashion and carried a coil of heavy wire tucked inside his web belt. I offered him a cigarette as he stood ogling my plane. After a moment he blurted the same question my father had asked so long ago: "You fly this machine, lootenant?"

I nodded. "What's with the wire?"

He looked puzzled. I indicated the coil at his waist.

"Oh. For the gooks underground. Make a noose, fish for 'em. Get 'em around the neck, haul 'em up, cut their throats." His gaze was still on the Corsair. "Jeez, lootenant, I'd be scared t'fly somethin' like that."

I laughed — air is air and ground is ground and never the twain shall savvy the other's job requirements. "Sarge," I said, "like the bus driver says, you can leave the flying to us. You just go ahead and fight the war."

He ambled off and I walked over within earshot of Doc who was talking earnestly with Brig. Gen. Lewie G. Merritt, the senior Marine officer on the island — he was pointing at a twin-engine PV-1 parked off the runway and insisting that it be assigned to lead us through possible storms on the over-water flight to Funafuti. He was within his rights, the transport plane with its full range of navigational equipment was available for fighter escort missions (fighters had only radios and dead reckoning plotting boards), but the general denied his request, saying he needed it on Tarawa. Then we don't go, said the Skipper. It could cost you your command, retorted the general. Okay Sir, said Doc, but I won't take twenty-four fighters seven hundred miles across the equator without it.

Grimly deadlocked, the two entered the command tent beside the airstrip. Ten minutes later Doc emerged and gave us a thumbs up — he'd gotten us our escort plane. Within the hour we were in the air again and we made our hop into the southern hemisphere without incident.

Doc Everton had long since earned our respect as a man and a leader of men and now we'd seen him put his career on the line rather than expose his fliers to what he knew could be trouble. We had reason to recall this one afternoon two weeks later when Lt. John Hansen of VMF 422 landed at Funafuti and reported that he'd become separated from the squadron in typhoon-strength line squalls on the way down from Tarawa, the same flight we'd made. Maj. John MacLaughlin, 422's Annapolis graduate commander, was a Stateside aviator who lacked Doc's experience; among other preparational oversights, he'd neglected to ask for an escort plane. Hansen, flying alone and monitoring the Gilberts frequency of 6970 kilocycles, had cranked his coffee-grinder receiver around and picked up the Funafuti radio range, and after more than five hours in the air he had touched down with 80 of his original 350 gallons of fuel remaining. He was the only one to get through, and he had no idea what had happened to the others.

We found out in the next few days. As a result of pyramiding errors of omission, an overlooked (possibly unseen) last-minute weather report, incomplete radio aids data and failures in inter-island communication, our sister squadron had suffered a disaster that launched one of the most extensive search-and-rescue operations of the Pacific war.

Up to their arrival at Tarawa their trip south had duplicated ours — they'd boarded a carrier in Pearl Harbor and been catapulted for the flight to the Helen airstrip. Next day, January 25, two hours after their take-off for Funafuti, they'd entered a weather front, lost their bearings and broken formation. Their flight plan, such as it was, called for a gas-up stop at Nanomea, the northernmost of the Ellice Islands, and they'd hit the front only 15 minutes short of it. Scattered in buffeting winds and blinding rain, Hansen became separated from his flight leader, Capt. John Rogers, and another division mate, Lt. Jake Wilson. Jake, flying alone, found a break in the weather over Niutao atoll, landed in the lagoon and was taken ashore by natives. Hansen got on the Funafuti beam and stayed with it through the storm.

At this point Lt. Chris Lauesen, with the main body of 20 planes led by Maj. MacLaughlin, radioed that his engine was cutting out. Curly Lehnert followed him down, watched him land, saw he was having problems with his life raft and bailed out to help him. By the time he had his own raft inflated, Lauesen and his plane had disappeared beneath 20-foot waves. Curly was alone in the storm-torn ocean.

The remaining 18 flew on through the raging front and in the next half hour several others, including Maj. MacLaughlin, went down out of fuel or disappeared into the clouds. Lts. Tommy Thompson, Ted Thurneau and Bill Aycrigg were seen to land in the ocean. Lt. Bob "Tiger" Moran was listed as missing until, some days after the search was terminated, we learned from natives on Nui island that he had parachuted over the beach, gotten tangled in his shroud lines and drowned in the surf before they could reach him in their canoes. They recovered his body and laid it ceremoniously to rest in their village burial ground.

Battered, exhausted and low on gas himself, Capt. Rex Jeans, a Guadalcanal veteran now in squadron command, made the only decision possible; he ordered the 13 pilots still in formation to form a traffic pattern over the sea, land as close together as possible and lash their rafts together. This was accomplished without further loss of life but with some very close calls. Lt. Mark "Breeze" Syrkin barely made it into his raft ahead of a shark. Chick Whalen, one of the last in the pattern, struck his head on landing and was floundering helplessly when Lt. John "Abe" Lincoln caught a glimpse of him on the crest of a comber, cut himself loose from the group, paddled over and pulled him into his raft. Chick, half conscious and thoroughly panicked, had stripped off his flight gear and clothes. When the last plane was down and all pilots roped together, Capt. Jeans took count — thirteen men in twelve rafts, several sick, some cut and bleeding, one naked to the elements. The storm showed no signs of abating, the seas roared down on them like loose freight cars on a steep grade. He noted that Syrkin's shark had been joined by two more and all three were circling his tiny flotilla. He was trying to think what to do next when suddenly Lt. Don Walker broke into song — "It ain't gonna rain no more no more, it ain't gonna rain no *more*" ... " In that moment he knew he and his lads were going to make it.

Walker's optimistic weather forecast didn't hold up, however, for it rained and blew and thundered intermittently throughout the next two days and nights while they fought the Pacific ocean, drove sharks off with their pistols, munched malted milk tablets and raw portions of a seagull that landed on Capt. Charley Hughes' raft. Then in mid-afternoon while they were psyching themselves up for their third night at sea Abe Lincoln spotted a PBY Catalina amphibian in the distance. They released dye markers and fired flares. The plane turned away, then miraculously turned back and flew directly over them, waggled its wings, circled and dropped smoke bombs. It circled five times, then descended slowly and crash-landed in the swells, springing a leak in its hull.

It took him three hours to do it in the wind and heaving seas but

Lt. George Davidson and his crew of Navy Patrol Squadron 53 got the thirteen castaways on board. He was unable to take off with a hold full of men and seawater so he held the PBY's nose into the wind and radioed his position. USS *Hobby*, a destroyer on search duty several miles away, acknowledged the call, arrived just before dark, took everyone on board and, after trying unsuccessfully to tow it, sank the waterlogged Catalina by gunfire.

We of 113 were waiting when *Hobby* entered Funafuti lagoon the morning of January 29 and disembarked our buddies of 422. They'd been 53 hours in their rafts and they were suffering from nausea, salt water sores and expo-

John "Abe" Lincoln, Congaree Field, S.C. 1945.

sure. Still feeling the effects of his crack on the head, Chick was taken to the island hospital for treatment and observation. Jake Wilson, Ted Thurneau and Curly Lehnert (later decorated for his attempted rescue of Chris Lauesen) had already been rescued and when the search was called off next day VMF 422's losses added up to 22 aircraft and six pilots. Maj. MacLaughlin was one of the six. Listening to distress calls and watching his planes go down into the sea, he had turned his command over to Rex Jeans and flown off into the storm by himself, never to be seen again.

In these last two weeks of January, 1944, the Funafuti anchorage was packed with troop transports and warships preparing for Operation Flintlock, the initial strike into the Marshalls. The battle for Tarawa had launched the new Central Pacific offensive and the Flintlock task force would now sweep through the archipelago, take certain islands in the Marshall chain (we were not told which ones) and by-pass the rest. When it sailed we would follow it north to operate from airfields on the captured islands. Meanwhile our duties consisted of draining oil strainers and warming up our engines for ten minutes every morning, leaving us with a lot of time on our hands. Released from hospital, Chick seemed subdued; in fact, anguish and frustration lay heavy on us all for we had lost planes and men in a combat zone without firing a shot — if winning a war depended on making fewer mistakes than the enemy, as conventional wisdom had it, we felt we'd already lost ours. We spent our days searching for "cats eye" stones along the ocean reef and striking up conversations with the Polynesian natives who talked to us in missionary English and awed us by the dignity with which they maintained their gentle customs among throngs of noisy Americans crowding their island.

Other fighter squadrons were arriving from Samoa, Wallis and Tutuila to take part in the Flintlock expedition, and shortly before the fleet sortied we joined the newly-arrived pilots in improvising a donnybrook that seems as improbable today as it did while it was taking place. It had started innocently enough one afternoon when a newcomer began bragging about the barhopping exploits of a flier in his unit, a Tennessee hillbilly who, he declared, was the most accomplished two-fisted drinking man in the U.S. Marine Corps. After taking a moment to consider this assertion, another man spoke up. "Don't misunderstand me, cousin," he said, "I'm not knocking your chap — perish the thought. What I'm saying is I'll bet hard dollars we got a flier in our outfit, fella from Texas we call the Siphon, who can drink your Tennessee yokel deaf, dumb and blind."

A gauntlet was on the ground. More were thrown down as others chimed in, each vaunting his squadron's ace tippler. Money began to show, a babble ensued:

"How we gonna find out who's top gun?"

"Yeah, we need somebody to organize a contest."

"We'll get old Earthquake McGoon, the air group athletic officer. He's a great organizer."

"McGoon? Hell, that dipshit couldn't organize a two-car funeral."

"Well then how about—"

"No, McGoon's our man, he's just dumb enough to make it go like it oughta. . ."

At first only the squadron champions were to be matched against each other, but after much palaver it was decided to hold a tournament with four contestants from each unit. These would be required to down a two ounce shot of Schenley's Black Label rye, known as "Black Death", every ten minutes; they could take it straight or mixed or standing on their heads but they had to be in their seats, unassisted, at the beginning of the next round. The last man sitting would be the winner.

With rules established for what would be known ever after as the Great Intersquadron Drinking Contest, a conference table was sneaked out the back door of the Flintlock headquarters building and moved into an empty fale, chairs set in place around it and a supply of whiskey laid in. These preparations were noted by passers by, news of interesting doings in the pilot area spread quickly across the island, and that night a crowd was gathering to place bets and cheer favorites when, at eight o'clock sharp, Referee McGoon blew a whistle to begin an affair the Funafutians would still be talking about at war's end.

I'd been running a fever for several days — Dr. Pierre "Pete" LaBorde, 113's Navy lieutenant flight surgeon, had diagnosed a touch of Dengue and prescribed abstinence — so I was watching from the sidelines as the ten-minute drinking bouts got underway with many toasts exchanged, much shouting and laughter and the inevitable bursts of song. There was a solo by one of the newcomers, a southerner by his accent, which many of us will never forget. A silence fell within the fale as he began singing a haunting Negro spiritual:

> . . . I want to be ready,
> I want to be ready, Lord,
> Walkin' through Jerusalem, just like John . . .

The hush lingered after he'd finished — we had few moments of beauty in our lives and they were deeply savored — then McGoon blew his whistle, John's long-ago trek through the Holy City gave way to a chorus of The Wabash Cannonball, and contestants got back to the business at hand.

Drinking had become general by this time and the wheels started coming off when one team's point man was kidnapped by a hit squad from another unit and released too late for the next round — betting odds fluctuated furiously and the aggrieved parties initiated a brawl in which the conference table was smashed flat. A player in a football game under the stars ran head first into a palm tree and was being revived at the moment some of our 113 fellows, returning from a joy-ride around the lagoon, missed the dock and drove their borrowed Navy launch up on the beach. The revels had reverted to the purpose which, consciously or not, everybody had in mind in the first place — to ease a little pre-combat tension and blow off emotional overload — and when they ended, long past the pumpkin hour, the Contest was a mere afterthought; there was nothing left of it except a few recumbent hard cases, no one standing, no sign of McGoon when it came time to declare the winners — the Texas Siphon and the Tennessee moonshiner. They sat in the middle of the fale floor, arms around each other's shoulders in happy oblivion. They glanced about at their demolished surroundings, then one said to the other: "Well, buddy, now that the rowdies has cleared out what say you and me have a peaceful little drink?"

Of all the memories of that night, however, one remains foremost in my mind. Heading back to our quarters, Dege and I made out a figure sitting alone on a log down by the shore. We recognized Chick and went over. His back was to us, I was about to speak, but something made me hold my tongue. He was slumped over, his head in his hands. He was weeping.

While we pilots were biding our time below the equator, our mates of the ground echelon were southbound out of Pearl Harbor on their way to meet us at a still-undesignated rendezvous. Scuttlebutt aboard the troop transport USS *Castor* was that they were headed for Truk, the Japanese naval base in the Carolines known as the Gibraltar of the Pacific, but in the pre-dawn murk of February 1 they found themselves among ships filing through a channel into a vast lagoon with palm-treed islets trailing off into the distance on either side. During the night they had joined the Flintlock task force off Kwajelein atoll in the heart of the Marshalls — they were out on the cutting edge of the Central Pacific invasion.

Kwajelein, with its 60-by-30 mile girth and 93 islands is the largest coral atoll in the world and it was where the Japanese had chosen to locate their mid-Pacific command center a quarter of a century earlier. They built two airfields, one at each end of its north-south axis, and both were being mercilessly pounded by Flintlock warships when *Castor* dropped anchor off the Roi-Namur island fighter strip in the northern sector — on the foredeck, listening to Naval gunfire directions on a communications jeep radio, our men watched whole groves of cocoanut trees lifted into the air and toppled like match sticks by 16-inch shells reducing the strip and its fortifications to a wasteland. The Tarawa lesson had been learned: battlewagons and cruisers were standing in close ashore and laying down a point-blank softening-up bombardment for swarms of troop-carrying LVTs and amtrac gunboats headed for the beaches.

Actually the Marshalls spearhead, massive as it appeared from *Castor*'s deck, was only part of a pan-Pacific strategy getting underway after months of planning at summit levels (most recently at the August meeting of the Joint Chiefs in Quebec) and in war rooms around the globe. It consisted of a giant whipsaw pincers, a right and a left hook thrown simultaneously — MacArthur's American and Australian troops pushing northward around New Guinea en route to the Philippines and Nimitz's fast carrier and amphibious task forces charging northwest through the mid-Pacific toward the Marianas and Okinawa. The captured islands, anchorages and airfields in the Marshalls were to be jumping-off points for the latter. To the south our people could see black clouds towering above another battle as units of the Army's 7th Division landed on the main island of Kwajelein. Far beyond the southeast horizon Majuro was also under attack, and plans called for the 4th Marine Division to move on to Eniwetok atoll, 325 miles to the west, after Roi-Namur was secured.

This happened sooner than expected; "Kwaj" had fallen quickly and on the stormy morning of February 17, three months ahead of the invasion schedule, *Castor* and her Flintlock companion ships entered Eniwetok lagoon. Eniwetok's geographic configurations were identical to that of the larger atoll — a fighter strip on the two-mile triangular island of Engebi in the northeast corner and a longer strip to accomodate bombers on the main island of Eniwetok in the south — but our ground contingent was not to have ringside seats for this show; word had been passed that they would go ashore on Engebi right behind the 22nd Regiment assault teams. They had no active participation assignment other than to establish a bivuoac area, but for them it was clearly the end of their travels, the last stop on the line. A Kwajelein-style bombardment had been going on since dawn, landing craft had hit the beach on schedule, and with one eye on the raging battle inland they spent the afternoon rechecking their 782 combat gear and waiting for the order to scramble down the landing nets into the boats.

It came at sunset; LVTs carried them ashore, they stumbled to high ground in darkness and took what shelter they could find in shell craters and Japanese slit trenches some two hundred yards beyond the beach. While tracer fire streaked around them, Sgt. Sullivan's Boom Room crew ate their K rations on their bellies with their chins in the dirt, and when they were finished Sully drew on his Cactus experience to instruct them concerning the night ahead. "There'll be infiltrators," he said, "there'll be a lot of shooting. Keep low and don't move. Don't let them spook you when they get close — the surest way to depart this world in a hurry is to stand up and start running around. . ."

The advice was good; shortly after midnight a grenade was lobbed into a nearby bivouac area, its people stampeded, a Nambu machinegun chattered in front of them and several were seen to fall. As our men were crawling out at first light to help pick them up they discovered a naked and terrified stranger cowering in their midst. "Kill the Jap bastard!" someone shouted. Sully intervened, ordering that he be bound and taken to the beach for questioning by Flintlock intelligence (it turned out the "Jap" was a non-combatant Korean laborer). A few minutes later a sweep of the area revealed that the Nambu had accounted for 17 American lives.

Engebi was declared secure that day, the assault teams withdrew and our men began the nauseous job of making their area habitable, collecting live ordnance and burying enemy dead, most of them in bits and pieces. For the next several days they slept under shelter halves, washed in the lagoon, ate with one hand and fanned flies away

Gunner Lewis Alexander with his homemade washing machine — plunger comprised of three Jap infantry helmets. Engebi, 1944. (his "reconditioned" Jap scooter is in the background.)

from their food with the other. The worst of it was the stench of death all around them, then it was the flies and the inability to get the grime off their bodies. After much futile spadework they finally dynamited their way down through coral and limestone to fresh water, lowered a pump into the hole and luxuriated in a mass hosing, their first decent wash-up since leaving the ship. But there was no escaping the flies or the smell.

The morning before our arrival at Engebi they were diverted by one of those wartime anomalies that were always cropping up in the midst of whatever was going on at the moment. Seabee bulldozers were filling in shell holes and preparing the landing strip to receive our planes when a lone F6F fighter appeared out of nowhere and swept low over the island with the obvious intention of landing. Our men had not been told that the Eniwetok invasion had been timed to coincide with a Navy Task Force 58 strike on Truk far to the west (the bombing nearly killed top Marine ace, Maj. Gregory "Pappy" Boyington, who had been shot down and captured by the Japanese the week before) and so could not know that the plane was off a carrier retiring from that attack. While they followed it with astonished eyes the Seabee crewchief ran out on the field and waved his dozers off to the edge of the runway. The fighter landed, rolled to a stop. With his engine running the pilot leaned out of the cockpit, scanned the crowd gathering around him and shouted, "Where's Doc Everton?"

Someone yelled, "He's not here yet."

"Too bad," he yelled back, "I've got a present for him. But you guys look like you could use it." He lifted a large carton from his cockpit well and handed it down, then he taxied back to the head of the strip, took off and disappeared to the north.

The men never learned who he was or where he was going but they enjoyed the five gallons of vanilla ice cream he left behind.

At 1100 the following day we had our first look at Engebi as Doc led us around it in tight squadron formation, circling once preparatory to breakup and landing. Task force ships crowded the lagoon below, Higgins boats thronged the beaches and dozers still scurried up and down the landing strip like beetles on a rotten log. We stared down at the triangular sea- encircled cornplaster that would be "Razor Base", our first permanent combat station. From a thousand feet in the air, with its coral surface pocked by explosives and its spikey topless palm trees scorched black by flamethrowers, it looked like the face of an unshaven pugugly after a bad night in the ring.

We circled several more times waiting for the dozers to clear the strip and, gazing down at the battered corner of a Marshall Island atoll, I thought of one of the legendary officers of the Marine Corps, the brilliant but unstable Lt. Col. Earle Ellis who, after serving with distinction in World War I, had become convinced that America was headed for a war with Japan and, in 1921, wrote a paper which became the basic Marine operational doctrine for it when it arrived. "Pete" Ellis was obsessed with the idea that the Japanese were fortifying islands in the Central Pacific. Posing as a civilian trading company executive, he arrived in Yokahama where, sick with nephritis and acute alcoholism, he wangled passage on a Japanese trader bounnd for the Marshalls. Months later authorities on Koror reported to Tokyo that he was dead. Cause of death was never learned, its circumstances remain a mystery to this day, and as we circled prior to landing on

Engebi that morning I wondered if the Corps' gutsy little strategic genius had investigated it twenty years ago, perhaps had his spy cover blown here.

What was certain was that we were here to stay — our shipboard mates were lined up along the parking area, cheering us as we landed and swarming all over us when we climbed down off the wing. Under the scorching tropical sun they appeared haggard after ten days of labor ashore but they were a joyous lot at that moment and they had much to tell us about their adventures as they shouldered our gear and led us up to our four-man Navy tents on the high ground. The last of the Jap dead were being buried in a mass grave nearby. Not all of them; in a grove behind the tent area we noted that two bodies, scorched naked and cindered to a crisp, still remained above ground in honorific testimony to their last hour on earth. They had been stacked together by some infantryman with a grisly sense of humor and a flair for landscape decoration — the penis of one was stuck in the ear of the other. Ground officer Russ Drumm laughed at our amazement. "Welcome to Engebi," he cried, "make yourselves at home!"

After a quick noon chow of C rations in the mess tent Doc called us together and outlined the present Razor Base tactical situation. We were under command of Marine Air Group 22, a skeleton staff of which was already here. An air warning system was aboard and its radar interception equipment would be operational by nightfall. VMF 422 with new planes and replacement pilots was expected shortly, as was VMSB-151, a dive bomber squadron flying SBDs, and an element of VMF(N)-532 flying radar-equipped Corsair night fighters. Until these units arrived we would be the only defensive air outfit on the atoll. Our duty consisted of protecting ships and ground installations against possible enemy attack which we would do by flying dawn-to-dusk four-plane combat air patrols, starting immediately — a flight schedule had been prepared and was posted in the ready tent beside the strip . . .

The Skipper paused and gave us one of his down-to-the- soles-of-the-feet stares. "Well, we're here," he said. "As of right now we're the point fighter outfit in the Central Pacific. You've been waiting for your chance a long time and. . ." He broke off. Picking up his briefing notes, his expression softened. "Okay, fellows," he added quietly, "it's all yours. Go to it."

Chapter Five

The official War Diary of Marine Fighting Squadron One Thirteen, which today gathers dust with hundreds of similar documents in U.S. Marine Corps archives in Washington, begins its monthly report for March, 1944, by tabulating unit statistics in a box headed by the single word STRENGTH:

Planes	22
Pilots	39
Ground O	10
Enlisted	241
USN O	1
USN Enlisted	8

The unit's twofold MISSION is set forth with all the pulse-racing vivacity of a drugstore prescription: *base defense and escort for long-range bombers.* Nonetheless, the dynamics inherent in these spare figures and flatfooted verbiage comprise the real story of VMF-113 — a complex, interactional story of some three hundred random individuals who were formed into a functionally effective combat organization by a wise and exemplary leader.

Simple long division shows that, beside the pilot who flew it, one F4U required a dozen highly trained men to keep it operating in a war environment, everything from mechanics, chute packers and explosives technicians to supply administrators, intelligence evaluators and bookkeepers. The eight enlisted personnel of "USN" were medical corpsmen; the "USN O" was their chief, Dr. Pierre Laborde, a wryly acerbic intellectual of South Carolina Huguenot descent who liked to splutter about "you goddam Marines, always getting yourselves into goddam pestholes like this one" yet who in his long Navy career invariably ended up in pesthole-bound Marine aviation units taking care of their people. "P-La-B" was a man of profound devotions and skin-deep disgruntlements, a crank and a humorist and the target of many a deprecatory wisecrack (during the cleanup of the island it was said that he wore flies on his face like generals wore combat ribbons on their chests), but when his services were required in the surgery tent he was what Marines called "good value".

Our operational departments were headed by the "Ground Os",

Marine gunners (warrant officers) and master sergeants, some of them expert in their service specialties and wondrously ingenious in the home-making arts. What they wanted and didn't have they built or fixed. As soon as our materiel officer, Gunner Lewis Alexander, had reconstructed a smashed two-cylinder Japanese engine to run a burned-out refrigeration unit he turned to devising a washing machine out of a packing- crate windmill, a Jap-helmet plunger and an oil-drum washtub. MTSgt. Delmar Lewis of the engineering department enlarged the original brakish water well and in a matter of hours had a pumping system and shower stalls in operation. A pile of lumber was discovered on the beach, screening was found somewhere and a pick-up team of carpenters knocked together an insect-free mess hall practically overnight. The order of the day was make-do-with-whatcha-got, the method was scrounge, and anything that wasn't nailed down was grist to the creative mill.

Sgt. Joe Gonzales inspecting the port landing gear of Corsair #55, "The Sudden Jerk."

First prize for Rube Goldberg tinkering, in my opinion, went to my plane captain on the Sudden Jerk, TSgt. Joe Gonzales, a wiry soft-spoken Louisianan who built a miniature distillation plant out of machine shop odds and ends

Navy doctor, Lt. Pierre LaBorde, "P-la-B," during cleanup after Engebi assault.

Lew Cunningham.

and began brewing up murderous batches of raisinjack in the corner of his tent. The Skipper got wind of this somehow, and what happened next became another of the many Doc Everton legends that the men of 113 still repeat to each other whenever they get together. He paid the tent a visit. Joe was not there. He took a quick look around, spotted the still in the corner, told Joe's tent mates he wanted to talk to Sgt. Gonzales and would be back in two hours. Joe returned to the tent and, hearing that the Old Man had come around looking for him, surmised that the raisinjack jig was up and that he had been given two hours of grace in which to get rid of the evidence. He dismantled the still and hustled it off to the garbage dump.

Doc arrived on the dot and glanced at the empty corner. "You wanted to see me, Sir?" Joe stammered, his knees knocking together.

Doc treated him to the paint-blistering stare, then turned to leave. "Nothing special, Joe," he said over his shoulder, "just wanted to know how you were getting along." The matter was dropped forthwith.

Actually Doc and the rest of us on the flight roster had little time for domestic matters for to execute the base defense half of our mission (the long-range bombers we were assigned to escort had not yet arrived) we were flying a dawn- to-dusk combat air patrol of two to four planes over Eniwetok ground installations and rear guard Flintlock ships still in the anchorage. Also, as our strength statistics show, we were two planes and one pilot short of full complement. At Makin Island, where we'd gassed up on the way north from Funafuti, Lew Cunningham and Charlie Prather were grounded with mechanical problems and we'd had to leave them behind. Lew rejoined us three days later but Charlie crashed on a test hop and we suffered our first operational pilot fatality since we'd lost Duff at El Toro. The War Diary entry for March 2 reads:

> DIED; Prather, Charles E., 2nd Lt., USMC.
> While attempting to land plane, plunged
> into water 50' short of runway and burst
> into flames. Not result of own misconduct.
> Body interred in Gate of Heaven Cemetery,
> Makin Island, Gilbert Group.

Quiet, thoughtful Charlie Prather had come to 113 as an enlisted pilot and received his commission at El Toro. Dege and I didn't know him as well as some others did, but he was one of us and we all mourned his passing. It was a sad and lonely place for a good man to go to rest.

Our CAP over ships and shore facilities was monitored constantly by Air Warning Squadron One which had been setting up its equipment the afternoon we arrived and was responsible for maintaining a 24-hour track of all aircraft in the area. A fighter director at the radar console kept our planes aloft informed of aerial activity, with particular attention to the southwestern approaches to the atoll beyond which lay the Jap-held Caroline Islands. Our intelligence officer Jack Morrison had briefed us on the nearest of these; his recon photographs showed that Ponape (Pon-a-pay), 370 miles distant, had a deep-water ship basin, one fully operational airfield and another under construction. A few hundred miles beyond Ponape was the great naval bastion of Truk. We were in the van of the situation Doc had described to us in California — American forces on the attack at last, poking up into enemy-held territory, forcing the Japs back toward their homeland. To meet their inevitable retaliatory attacks we maintained not only a daylight-hours fighter umbrella but eight back-up aircraft standing by on the deck, all manned and ready to scramble at the first growl of the air raid siren.

For all of us who were there at the time, some of those monosyllabic War Diary entries project whole technicolor worlds on memory's screen, and the one concerning March 7 does it for me by noting that my wingman Al Little and I flew the dusk CAP. Indeed we did: that evening we cruised at low r.p.m. in a glorious Central Pacific sunset with cumulus cloud towers on every hand flamed by pink and saffron shafts of light while the lagoon, two miles below, turned slowly from cerulean to deep cobalt. I remember we had a few tense moments early in our watch when the director vectored us out to intercept a suspicious blip on his scope, a single plane closing the area. We charged our guns, fired test bursts and raced to meet the bogey, which turned out to be an Army R4D from Roi-Namur who'd forgotten to turn on his IFF identification signal. We made a hairy head-on pass at his nose to drive home what could happen to him in bad visibility as a result of his oversight, then we returned to station and spent another hour droning along through darkening cloud corridors above the tiny toy ships in the anchorage.

Flying CAP was tedious and nerve-racking duty for we could not depend entirely on ground control to warn us of incoming trouble. Doc repeatedly cautioned us to stay alert: "Your neck's a universal joint," he said, "keep your eyes out of the cockpit, keep looking around, you never know when they'll sneak in or where they'll come from." The schedule was onerous, the threat was there; Al and I were eager to meet it, and if we'd seen nothing of the enemy in our first week of watchful waiting we were sure he'd be showing up in his own good time. We could not know it, of course, but that evening the time was near.

We'd learned to recognize each of our fighter directors by his voice; on this flight we had the talkative one, an easy- going, relaxed type. At its end he came on the air once more: "Razor four zero from Razor Base. Anything happening up there?"

I laughed. "You should be telling us."

"Nothing on the scope. Pretty sunset?"

"Gorgeous."

"How about you, four one — enjoying yourself?"

Al grinned over at me as he picked up his hand mike to reply. "More fun than anything else I could do with my clothes on."

I looked at my wrist watch. "About time for the fat lady to sing, Razor Base."

"Roger, four zero, your nighthawk relief's warming up, you're clear to come home. Razor Base out."

It was almost dark when we landed and taxied to the scramble line. We switched off, unhooked our safety harnesses and climbed down just as one of the eight recently-arrived night fighters of VMF(N)-532 was taking off. These Corsairs were equipped with a small air intercept radar set with a scope in the cockpit and a streamlined scanner at the tip of the starboard wing. When a bogey appeared on the Razor Base radar the pilot would take his first long-range vector from the fighter director, then, closing his target from the rear, he would track it on his cockpit set until he was near enough to make out its black silhouette in his gunsight. It was tricky work and, standing by our planes, we watched admiringly as this first nighthawk of March 7-8 soared up clear of the runway and disappeared into the stars.

Lugging our chutes across the strip we could hear shouts of a volleyball game still in progress in the tent area. Al touched my elbow and nodded at a full moon rising above the maintenance shed. "It'll be good to have those guys up there tonight," he said.

Al "Sparrow" Little, my staunch and splendid wingman.

Al, a jolly Californian with a skinny neck that had earned him the nickname "Sparrow," was one of several new pilots replacing original El Toro hands who had been transferred out of the squadron because of health problems, promotions in rank or other reasons. He'd started out a bit shaky on my wing but he was settling down. I had nothing to add to his comment. We hung our chutes and flight gear in the ready tent and walked up the slope to the mess hall where the cooks would be holding supper for us.

Dege, Z.O. Humphreys, ground officer Augie Goetz and I shared a four-man tent and we bunked in early that night, which was just as well for the air raid siren began its hysterical roller-coaster wail at 0332 in the morning. Its previous rude awakenings had been false alarms so we took our time responding to this one. In the dark I heard Dege open the metal ammo box in which we kept our meager rations of Lucky Lager on ice scrounged from Alex's refrigerator. A can popped, his Zippo flared to light a cigarette. Wordlessly we pulled on shirts, pants and boondockers, stumbled through the tent flaps and went outside. The sky was cloudless and bright with the moon hanging half way down in the west.

The siren quieted and silence fell on the camp — no flashlights poking around, no voices or sounds of any sort. We sat on sandbags rimming the mouth of our foxhole and scanned the sky overhead which appeared vacant as a ward-heeler's promise. Twenty minutes passed. Dege, half asleep, yawned, crumpled his beer can and threw it away. As though in response, Augie grumbled, "Another phony! I'm going back to the sack."

He'd risen to his feet and had taken a step toward the tent when the night suddenly erupted with the whomping of our five-inch anti-aircraft guns emplaced around the strip, instantly followed by a series of banshee screams and ground- shuddering explosions. Augie let out a yell and we scrambled down into our hole before he dove in on top of us.

That first string of bombs knocked out our ground radar system and radio communication with the night fighters aloft. The bombers (types and numbers were never known) then came down low and, braving our ack ack guns at 500 feet, wreaked havoc for the next hour and a half. Again and again their 1000-pound daisy-cutters stitched Engebi from end to end. One landed in the ammunition dump which went up in a Vesuvius detonation that shook the island like a terrier shakes a rat.

Down in our hole, faces in the dirt, we sweated out the minutes between runs. We could feel them coming — each time we'd hear the faint hum of engines as they regrouped in the distance, the hum becoming louder, becoming a snarl then a roar as the sandbagged aperture above our heads lit up bright as day with streaking 40 mm. tracers, orange shellfire blossoms and ground concussions that tossed showers of coral dust in our faces and down our necks. At one point we heard the bullhorn voice of Adjutant Smith in the role next to ours rise above the racket overhead. As we learned later, Tom Kalhorn had asked the old Cactus hand if the Canal had been any worse than this, whereupon Smitty, who we called "The Great White Father," threw back his head and howled, "Only God can save us now !..."

Curled fetus-fashion in the dark, surrounded and half suffocated within the hellish rattling crescendo of falling bombs, we lost count of the passes (actually there couldn't have been more than three or four) but the time-over-target was easily ascertained; it's right there in the record for all to see: *one and a half hours from first drop to last. . .*

We lay still for several minutes after the all-clear sounded, not quite believing it was over. We could hear the muffled crump of ammunition still cooking off in the dump at the end of the island, then voices, tentative shouts, people moving around above our heads. One by one we crawled out and stood staring stupidly at the carnage. Secondary fires flickered everywhere, several tents had been blasted to shreds by bomb fragments. A flashlight was coming our way, probing its beam into foxholes. It stopped at ours and blinded us as it played from face to face. The stumpy figure holding it said, "All okay here?"

Z.O. found his voice. "All okay, Skipper."

Doc grinned, his eyes bulging as they did when he was angry or worried. "You've had a taste of it," he said, and moved on.

Our tent was untouched so we joined in the clean-up efforts of those not so lucky. We'd had no casualties in the pilot area but there was plenty of damage, bits of splintered tent poles and canvass strewn about, foot lockers blown open and their contents scattered — our corner of the island looked more like a direct hit on a military surplus store than a battle area campground. As in even the most somber of our collective situations, though, there

Capt. Bill Letts and his bomb-blasted saxophone.

were laughs. After much searching in the dark Capt. Bill Letts discovered what was left of his beloved saxophone in a tangle of shirts and socks half way across the compound — it had been blasted into a twisted blob of silver metal. Bill displayed it with a cardboard sign demanding, *What are YOU fighting for?*

By sunrise an island-wide damage assessment survey was well along. Considering the enemy's persistence and accuracy, casualties were light: one dead, seven wounded. In the middle of the attack Dr. LaBorde had been summoned to assist another surgeon in amputating an enlisted man's shrapnel-mangled foot. He told the story in typically choleric P-La-B fashion for he was convinced the fellow's foot could have been saved if he'd been called sooner — the operation had gone too far by the time he arrived and they'd had to take it off. We were worried about our 50.calibre ammunition supply, over 400 boxes containing 115,000 rounds, whereupon Sgt. Sullivan revealed that he and Gunner Garner had done their worrying prior to the event; two days before they'd had the Boom Room crew take the boxes from the ammo dump and stash them around the island in a number of well separated holes. They were all intact and VMF-113 was still in the war.

The question arose: where were the night fighters, why didn't they get the bandits before they blew up our ground radar? The answer the air warning squadron people gave was "window", the code word for bundles of strip metal the Japanese threw out of bombers approaching a target to confuse radar signals — the clouds of metal chaff had fogged the scopes and defeated attempts to put the nighthawks onto targets before the first bombs fell. After that they had no ground direction at all.

Miraculously, damage to the air strip and planes along the flight line was minimal and we were back on a regular schedule of operations within hours. It had been a true baptism under fire, however, and residual tension was everywhere in comic evidence. That noon a sheet of corrugated metal slid off a truck near the mess hall and the clatter of its ground impact sent a hundred men in the chow line racing for their foxholes. The whine of a Corsair on final or the reverberations of a spanner dropped on a metal bench caused all within earshot to throw themselves face down in the dirt.

Cpl. Buchwald caught the aftermath spirit in his next edition of

THE U-MAN COMEDY: "During the raid every foxhole was transformed into a church, sins were recalled, enemies forgiven, debts forgotten, and since that night men have taken to sleeping fully clothed with their boots on ... Do you suffer from bomb raids? Does shrapnel get in your hair? Don't let it bother you. Just run like hell for the nearest hole, cuddle up in a little ball and pray for all you're worth . . ."

Although it was not discussed out loud, many of us pilots were gripped by another species of trauma in the wake of that first bombing raid. It was emotional rather than panic-impulsive and it was subtler, slower to take effect. It seemed to be located in the gut, something like a nagging case of heartburn, but its origin was not physiological; it was frustration over being so long on the receiving end of hostilities. Since we'd come south we'd lost lives and airplanes, we had nothing to say for ourselves, nothing even that would justify our existence as a fighting team, and here we were flying around in empty skies all day waiting for an enemy that came at night to drop their bombs unhindered while we grovelled helplessly underground. We knew that Ponape was where he came from but Ponape was beyond the F4U's tactical range and we couldn't get at him.

This was a particularly low time for me. The next afternoon, flying CAP with Larry Johnson as wingman, I spotted a large boat or small ship aground on the seaward edge of an islet along the east side of the atoll. I hadn't noticed it before, nor had anyone reported it, so I signalled Larry that we were going down to take a look.

On the first pass we could see that its bow had been torn out on the coral reef — it was a wreck, all right, and from the rust around its torn undersides it appeared to be an old one, long abandoned. We dropped down to 100 feet, cut back on power and dropped flaps to see if we could make out the ship's name or registry.

Larry was another green replacement pilot, he was on my port wing as we came in, and for some reason he decided to cross over to starboard astern of me. It was a crazy thing to do at slow speed and low altitude and before I could get on the radio to stop him he was flying through my slipstream, whereupon he staggered into a nosehigh stall, swung sickeningly off to the side and tumbled onto the reef, tearing his starboard wing clear of the fuselage.

Pouring on the power and circling, I saw him climb out of his cockpit and stand on the coral. He'd at least had the good sense to lock his belt and safety harness before dropping his flaps, which enabled him to survive the crash with only a lacerated scalp. He waved up at me and I rocked my wings, indicating I had him in sight, was reporting his position and would return to base to send help.

An hour later, after a Higgins boat had been dispatched to pick him up, I told the Skipper what had happened. We stood outside his command tent, the sun was low on the horizon and I was sweating inside my flight suit. Doc listened closely to my account, studying my face. When I'd finished he took a moment to think it over. Then he nodded.

"It's okay, Available," he said, "I get the picture. It's too bad, but these things happen." He looked at me. "How are you feeling?"

I told him I was feeling fine, but it was a lie. Although my C.O. had exonerated me of blame, I'd still been the leader of a patrol that had taken off with two planes and landed with one. The truth was I felt terrible.

On top of this, word was going around that Pop Flaherty, recently promoted to major, was being transferred to a squadron in SoPac as its executive officer — it was not official, no orders had been received, but he was due for a raise and Dege and I, who'd been in his wedding and had flown in his division since El Toro days, offered premature congratulations. It was clear that his departure would create a crisis because Pop, along with Frank Drury and Huck Watkins, had been hand-picked by Doc; he was an old Guadalcanal vet the Skipper depended on for leadership within the squadron. Those of us junior men who were not so junior any more would be required to lead four-plane divisions and assume other responsibilities beyond our rank.

The crisis was exacerbated by a dumb caper three of us pulled while on a detached flight at Kwajelein. We'd had the morale-boosting news that the Army's 48th Bomber Squadron had landed B-25s on Eniwetok and was ready to hit Ponape, also that external fuel tanks which would give our F4Us the legs we needed to escort them down and back were waiting for us at Roi-Namur. The tanks were a droppable type that had to be fitted to toggles on the underbody of each plane. The action order was to fly down to Roi in rotation — half the squadron to Roi while the other half did double duty keeping watch over

Razor Base — pick up the empty tanks and bring them back. When everybody had tanks we'd be ready to fill them up and fly southwest on our first strike into the Carolines.

In the landing approach over Kwaj lagoon our group flew over a Navy freighter disembarking several boatloads of supplies on the Roi beach, and on the ground we learned that one of the boats was jammed to the bulkheads with cases of Lucky Lager. Dege, Lew and I took counsel and decided to purchase a few cases from the commissary sergeant to supplement our beer supply on Engebi. But transportation was a problem — there wasn't enough cockpit space for more than a few cans. I forget which one of us came up with the solution: since we were going to fly these brand new belly tanks back home empty, why not buy a jeep load of the stuff, drive it down to the flightline and. . ?

We waited until dark to execute the plan. On the line we drew straws to see who would be the cargo carrier. Dege drew short and we spent the next two hours cracking cans of Lucky Lager and pouring the contents into his belly tank.

We took off the following morning and joined up in formation while climbing on a westerly heading for Engebi. Dege was leading the second section of the tail end division and all went well with him until we hit some bumpy turbulence at seven thousand feet, at which point a thin white stream of beer foam started spewing from his tank's overflow pipe — Dege himself was unaware of it but Lew and I watched in consternation as our investment drained away to the last drop in a gossamer haze descending on the Pacific below.

Of course the story went through the squadron with the speed of light, giving rise to great merriment and making Degan, Cunningham and Jones the collective butt of much jocularity. That night Doc called us into his tent. He sat behind his desk, we stood at attention in front of it. It might be said in our defense that the thought of going down and blowing up Ponape had put us in overly high spirits, even turned us a bit light in the head, but it was immediately apparent that the Skipper was having none of this. After thirty seconds of the cruel stare he spoke: "Do you fellows want to go home?"

Go home? The question stunned us speechless. I couldn't believe I'd heard it. My stomach rolled over, the flesh of my arms and shoulders burned like fire. Finally Lew managed to stammer a reply:

"No Sir. . . *No Sir!*"

The staring silence a moment longer. Then, "Okay. As you know, Pop is expecting orders, he's leaving the outfit. Tomorrow we go on the offensive. Whether you realize it or not, these new pilots look up to you three men. I can't have a bunch of clowns leading divisions, I expect more from you than crazy stunts. Do I make myself clear?"

The three of us in unison: "*Yes Sir!*"

Doc dismissed us with a nod and we filed out of the tent without a word.

We never hashed over this confrontation because there was no need — each of us, through our knowledge of the man, had grasped its real import. The question about going home was to startle some sense into us. The Skipper didn't want to get rid of us; he wanted us to shape up. Loyalty goes down as well as up and he was putting us on our metal, offering a challenge. He'd said it himself, he'd spelled it out — he said he expected more from us. He could have sent for pilots who flew as well as we did, he could have gotten men further along in the war business than we were, but he didn't want that: he wanted *us* . . .

Which was nice, but it went further; it meant that he knew we wouldn't fail him, and *that* meant that *we* knew it too.

Chapter Six

At dawn next morning, those of us on the day's CAP schedule stood watching as sixteen of our Corsairs took off to join ten B-25s in an attack on Ponape. It was our first escort-type expedition and a new experience in almost every aspect, starting with target topography. Since Hawaii we'd seen only flat, palm-tassled islets and coral reefs strung around atoll lagoons. Mountainous Ponape, by contrast, was a solid 130-square mile volcanic mass with waterfalls like threads of quicksilver stitching down through vast slopes of rain forest from 3000-foot peaks. Approaching it from aloft, it loomed dark and brooding with its lower flanks swathed in clouds, an impregnable, monolithic presence standing alone in the surrounding sea.

The island's history was as eerie as its mien. Discovered in the 17th century and claimed for the Spanish crown, its explorers found ruins of a prehistoric civilization, a series of sea-level forts linked by canals and manned by legendary warriors their Micronesian descendents insisted were nine feet tall. Spain sold it to Germany in 1899 and the Germans built a town fronting on the harbor at its eastern end. After World War I it was mandated to the Japanese who immediately set about building an airfield in a valley between two mountain ridges — and, as Jack Morrison told us, they were presently hard at work building another.

Coming at it from the north that morning, the attackers flew through a flak screen which Doc described in his action report as intense but ineffective, "accurate for altitude but inaccurate for sighting" — that there was an AA pattern in the sky before their arrival, however, revealed that the Japs had an operative radar warning system. There were no aircraft on either field, so as soon as the B-25s dropped their bombs and left the target zone our fliers descended to treetop level and shot up every defensive gun emplacement they could find. Racing east out of the valley they got a good look at the old German Ponape town — they told of red-roofed buildings and white, presumably concrete streets. One man swore he saw a movie theater with a marquee but went by it too fast to make out what was playing.

The kicker came that afternoon when 48th Bomber Command on

Eniwetok reported that while turning for home one of its pilots had spotted three Zero-type aircraft in the distance off the south coast of the island. *Zeros!* We'd never seen a Zero, we'd never expected to encounter Zeros in this area, and the mere possibility that there might be enemy fighters in it was another electrifying novelty. The Skipper questioned each member of the flight individually — had he seen anything anywhere in the sky that looked even vaguely like a Zero? No Sir, nothing. Think hard, man, *nothing at all?* Nothing, Skipper...

Most of us thought the Army was blowing smoke, but Doc was taking no chances. He flew down to the main island, personally grilled the pilot who'd made the sighting and drew up plans for a strike the next day with the bomber group C.O. He came back after dark, called us all together in the ready tent and gave us the drill.

His attack plan involved two elements operating independently. "I'll go down with Frank's division escorting four bombers," he said. "The rest of you, less those on CAP duty, will go with nine bombers. My six will come in low and sweep the field like we did today, and you people with the main bomber group will go in high. We know they have radar down there and if they have Zeros they'll probably be up at altitude to intercept your group. My six will flush out any birds still on the deck." Morrison gave us the updated information he'd gleaned from the morning's debriefing and for half an hour we restudied the island photographs and topo maps, immediately after which we packed in. Take off was scheduled for 0700.

It seemed that only a few minutes had passed since we'd doused the single-bulb in our tent before the sergeant of the guard was shaking us awake — my wrist watch read 0510. Ground officer Augie Goetz woke while Dege, Z.O. and I were pulling on flight suits and lacing boondockers in the dark. He grunted, raised his head, muttered the traditional good luck greeting between theater people — "Break a leg, fellows" — rolled over and went back to sleep.

We stumbled across the compound under the stars, ate dehydrated scrambled eggs and gulped hot coffee in the bleary illumination of the mess shack, then followed our flashlights down the slope to the ready tent. Some of the strike pilots were already there putting on their flight gear, others followed us inside. There was much grunting and bumping into each other in the semi-darkness but little conversation. Psych-up time was not for talk. Preparation for an attack was profoundly personal, a few moments of introspection during which the hands were kept busy buttoning and zipping while the imagination wandered among dire possibilities and the spirit gathered its resources. Some reassurance came from handling familiar objects — the little dye-marker packets on the collar of the Mae West, the hefty holstered .45 nestled at the left armpit, the big survival knife-machete slung snug on the right hip. It wasn't much, but it was something, and we made the most of it.

Lugging chutes, we trooped out onto the strip. The brilliant starpoints of the Southern Cross, lying on its side over the tent area, were fading in a graying sky and, approaching the flight line, I could make out my friend Joe Gonzales waiting beside Corsair #55.

"Morning, lieutenant," he said shyly in his songsong Louisiana lilt. "Gonna be a good day."

"Fine day, Joe. The Jerk ready to go?"

"All ready."

Climbing up on the wing behind me, Joe bent over the cockpit and helped me strap in — he was quiet, cheerful as ever, offering no special good wishes or giving any outward sign that he considered this morning's operation higher in pucker-factor than a routine patrol. He jumped down while his assistant, Sgt. Randal Bennish, dragged the fire extinguisher up near the exhaust ports under the nose. I nodded at both men and switched on. The starter whined, the prop blades swung slowly, the engine kicked, snuffled, then caught with a roar, and I started working my way down the check-off list.

I glanced right and left along the line where my flight mates, featureless specters hunched over their cockpit lights, were doing the same thing. Lonely time now. I remember I thought of a quote I'd read in a story by William Faulkner about a boy, an old Indian and an enormous male bear of mythic repute that roamed the forests of Mississippi early in the century. Old Ben, the idea of Old Ben, obsessed the boy, he sought him constantly in the high timber, and his woodsman mentor, the wise Chickasaw Sam Fathers, knew that some day he would find him. Sam had some advice for him when he did: "*Be scared. You can't help that. But don't be afraid. Ain't nothing in the woods going to hurt you if you don't corner it or it don't smell that you are afraid. . .*"

For some reason Sam's words struck me funny that morning. I was going sweaty-palmed into the woods, I'd probably smell like a musk ox in rut, but I wasn't going to corner anything up there in the big sky — if I found Old Ben among the clouds I'd just settle down nice and calm and blow him and his companion bears all to hell. . .

Check-off completed, I waggled a thumb at the crewmen, they pulled the chocks from my wheels and I rolled out to the head of the runway. Doc was already airborne (my watch showed 0655), his five sweepers were roaring one after the other down the strip and off into the gloom. Squadron executive officer Charlie Kimak, leading the 12-plane high escort, went next with his division. Pop, with Hap Haspell on his wing, led the second division; I led Pop's second section with wingman Al Little. We took off singly and joined up in a climbing turn.

The sun was topping the horizon when we located the B-25s at angels ten over Eniwetok and took positions on either side of them, with the last division still climbing to fly top cover. The bombers looked splendid, their tan fuselages gleaming in the dawn. There was a thin scrim of cirrus in the tropopause directly overhead, there was azure sky 360 degrees around the horizon — like Joe said, it was going to be a good day.

We throttled back to keep pace with the bombers, fattened prop pitch to save gas and switched to belly tanks. We had almost two hours to target, straight, level and silent on a southwesterly course. I looked around at the formation, singling out those who had started with us at El Toro — Ken Geelhood astern, Tom Kalhorn in the top flight, Joe Chrobuck on the other side of the bombers. I adjusted trim tabs and shrugged comfortably into my chute harness for the long pull.

The time passed slowly; then, right on schedule, the sullen peaks of Ponape materialied on the horizon above a heavy overcast shrouding valleys and lowlands. I was thinking of our sweepers down there beneath the clouds when suddenly our earphones crackled and I heard the Skipper's voice. Static garbled his words — breaking radio silence meant they were important, *damned* important, but I hadn't gotten the message. I looked over at Al. He was staring at me, worried; he hadn't gotten it either.

A minute later we heard it again, still garbled but we were closer now and a few words were distinguishable, something about Zeros. Charlie Kimak got on the net, asking for clarification. We all heard it this time, or part of it: ". . .Zeros aloft. . . Keep your eyes open. . . "

Hot damn, I thought, we're going to get into them!

Others expressed the same reaction over the air in an earsplitting rebel yell followed by a string of overlapping expletives:

"Son of a bitch!—"

"Where are they, anybody see them?—"

"Give 'em hell, sweepers, chew 'em up and spit 'em out!"

"Shit no, leave some for us!"

Charlie called for silence and gave the signal to prepare for action.

I switched to main gas tank and pulled the handle to release my external tank — as it fell free the Jerk leaped forward like Man-o-War out of the gate. Nodding at Al to loosen formation, I shoved the gas mixture knob and prop pitch forward into low, toggled gun switches, charged them and fired a test burst. We were all loosened up and unfettered now, scanning the sky in every direction, up and down. At full operational speed we had to initiate weaving patterns in order to stay close to the bombers as they soared in over the harbor and dropped their ordnance.

Black puffs of ack ack blossomed here and there but it was scattered fire, nowhere near us, obviously a random effort. We kept straining our eyes for a glimpse of enemy fighters. We saw the Army's bombs explode beneath the broken overcast, some in the harbor, a few on the shoreline — the pattern looked almost as ineffectual as the Jap flak screen — then the B-25s swung around in a lazy circle and headed for home. We followed, still hoping for action. . .

We had none, but that wasn't the whole story by a long shot. The fellows sweeping the airfield in the hills before our arrival had had plenty.

In those days there were two ways of becoming a Marine aviator. Most of us in 113 had come by the college boy route which required that a civilian applicant within the age bracket be unmarried, have passing grades in two years of higher education and straight A's on the Navy flight physical. The "flying sergeant" route was taken by enlisted three-stripers who had requested and been accepted for flight training. A couple of these enlistees, commissioned 2nd lieutenants upon graduation, were in the group of sweepers that morning — Bernie

Nelson, flying Doc's wing, and Pete Tunno on the wing of Texan Emmet Anglin. The others in the flight were old Cactus hand Frank Drury and lanky Joe Schellack from Oklahoma.

They were waiting for us of the main escort group when we landed back on Engebi shortly before noon. They were in a state approaching euphoria, which was not surprising since what they'd accomplished two hours earlier is cited in military histories as one of the classic aerial engagements of the Central Pacific war. The gunfight, recounted by them at the debriefing, sounded like high noon in Dodge City with half a dozen Gary Coopers doing the shooting.

With their four bombers they had approached the island from the southwest this time, flying in three two-plane sections at wavetop level (Doc's practise in our Pearl Harbor war exercises) on a magnetic heading of 040. They raced through rain squalls and a cloud front and were probably successful in sneaking under radar surveillance but they must have been sighted visually for they had to run a gantlet of heavy AA fire from the ridge above the airfield. They got through it unscathed and, skimming the ridge and diving into the valley, they beheld a fighter pilot's dream dead ahead in their gunsights — a whole squadron of Zekes, the type of Zeros encountered that day, in the process of scrambling off the deck.

As leader, Doc was the first within range. He blasted one lifting off the strip with its wheels half retracted, observed tracers sparking along its engine cowling and cockpit and saw it career away to the left out of his line of vision. He pulled up onto the tail of a second, hit it in the wingroot and watched it burst into flame, roll over and crash into the mountainside.

Doc was going after a third that was hightailing it out of the valley when his wingman Bernie Nelson went into action. Seeing a Zeke closing on his starboard quarter, Nellie yanked around in a hard evasive maneuver, shook it off his tail and lost sight of it. A second later he spotted another directly overhead, pulled up and squeezed off a burst, the recoil of which checked him dead in a hammerhead stall. Recovering from the spin, he saw a Corsair (Joe Schellack's) chasing a Zeke across the valley floor, joined the chase and blasted it. "I saw the guy turn around to look at me," he said, "but it was too late for him to get out of the way. His right wing exploded and he went cartwheeling end over end into the trees."

By this time — it could have been no more than 60 seconds since the Skipper fired his opening salvo — the airspace over the valley had become one great whirling maelstrom with six big blue-gray Corsairs and twice that number of sleek brown crimson-meatballed Zekes all climbing and diving among the mountains in a deadly effort to chew each other up.

Joe Schellack, high scorer of the Ponape victory.

The battle went against the hostiles from the outset. Drury blew one into the ground on his first pass. Schellack, who came away high scorer of the morning, dropped on the Zeke that had made the pass at Nelson, hit it at full deflection and watched it pull up into a stall — "it went straight up like it was shot from a bow!" he said — then it fell off, plunged nose-first into the trees and blew up in a monstrous fireball. He was pumping rounds into the tail of another when suddenly tracers started streaking past his starboard wingtip from astern — it was Nelson who'd just recovered from his spin, saw Joe going after his second target and decided to lend a hand. Joe and Nellie were each given a half credit for the kill.

Our people had achieved surprise and gotten the jump on the enemy, but it was unquestionably this kind of superb split-second teamwork that afforded them the victory. A few seconds after he and Nellie parted company, Joe saw a Zeke on Anglin's tail, called him on his radio and told him to turn toward him. Anglin turned sharply, the Zeke followed him and Joe hit it head on with a single short burst — its cowling and one wing flew off, it flipped over and turned into a smear of fiery wreckage tumbling across the ground. Good shooting also had much to do with the score.

Anglin and Tunno were the tail section of the attack, the last of the six into the valley. Anglin saw two Zekes at 1200 feet climbing away from the fracas, zoomed up after them and got in a burst at one before it disappeared into clouds. He saw another below him, dropped on it, smoked it and watched it crash. Pete Tunno played tag in and out of the clouds with a couple of Zekes, observed hits on one of them before it got away, robbing him of a confirmed kill. His Italian dander up, he turned and bore down on two 70-foot patrol craft in Ponape harbor, disintegrating one and shooting up the other. He came back to empty his ammo trays strafing the field, then joined up on Schellack who was heading for the rendezvous point over the small island of Jokaj east of Ponape. The others were already circling it waiting for them.

It was at this point that Doc radioed his warning to us coming in high with our bombers. He thought some Zekes might still be in the air to give us trouble. As it turned out he could have saved his breath — if there were any, they wanted nothing more to do with the planes they called "Whistling Death". As far as we were concerned, Doc and his team had finished them off.

By the end of the debriefing we were as elated as the intrepid six. With all our planes safely returned to base, the day's tally came to nine enemy aircraft destroyed and three probably destroyed, one patrol vessel sunk, one damaged. In a single beautifully planned and executed surprise attack, Skipper Everton, with two more meatballs on his fuselage, now ranked up with Marion Carl, Joe Foss, Ken Walsh, Col. John Lucien Smith, Pappy Boyington and other top Marine aces. The battle lasted between ten and fifteen minutes according to varying adrenalin-charged estimates, and in that wink of time he'd demonstrated the Beast's tactical superiority over the Zero and shown us we could hit live targets as well as wire mesh banners. We didn't think about it in these terms, of course; we thought in terms of Col. Joe Bauer's time-honored story about the two bulls on the hilltop — six of us had "walked down there and knocked 'em all off . . ."

In fact, we'd cleaned out the Ponape camp. We hadn't seen the last of Jap bombers overhead at night but the next ones to visit us staged up from Truk, well beyond our tactical reach, and went back to Truk when they were through. In our several subsequent raids against Ponape we never saw another Jap aircraft of any type.

We had a party that night. The whiskey supply we'd bought at

Above: *Air and ground crew officers of VMF-113 taken day after wiping out Ponape Zero Squadron (note Jap flags on insignia board).*

The Ponape raiders. Doc pasting up meatballs on the Engebi scoreboard. Kneeling: Pete Tunno, Bernie Nelson. Standing: Emmett Anglin, Frank Drury, and Joe Schellack.

Right: Shot of Doc Everton signing yellow sheet upon landing after Ponape victory — ground crewmen rejoicing over his two Zero victories.

At the post-raid party that night, intelligence officer "Pinkie" Morrison leads us in song.

Ewa which was supposed to follow us into the combat zone had not caught up with us, but Doc located a few bottles somewhere and we celebrated VMF-113's blooding with much raucous jollity. I had an old battered 80-bass accordian which I'd won in a poker game at Funafuti and I'd worked up a verse to the famous British-Australian ditty "Bless 'Em All":

> One Thirteen has arrived here today
> The colonels and group C.O.'s say
> We'll give 'em the C.A.P. to fly
> From dawn tomorrow 'till the day they die
> They'll eat shit-on-a-shingle and beans
> And to show them that we're on the ball
> We'll swipe all their gear
> And drink all their beer
> 'Cause we've got the rank, BLESS 'EM ALL...

We sang it for the first time that night and, after a couple of practise runthroughs, it sounded like a bar room rendition of the Hallelujah Chorus.

Today, half a century later, our eagerness to get at the enemy and destroy him may sound excessive, maybe even hard to believe, but it is not in the least exaggerated — destroying the enemy was the seldom-spoken purpose behind everything we'd been doing for the previous two years and it was at the very heart of our collective temperament. There was vengefulness in it for we'd seen the devastation he'd accomplished by sneak attack at Pearl Harbor and Ewa. If anything, we felt that our retaliation was better than he deserved; our photographs of the Ponape installations had been taken not by slant-eyed camera- toting Honolulu "tourists" but by reconaissance aircraft at high risk in wartime conditions; the Japs knew we were here, they'd thrown the first punch, and if we'd caught them unawares that morning as we'd planned to do, we'd beaten them fair-and- square by the grace of American industrial capacity, intensive training and superior performance in battle. We had what to us were very good reasons for feeling not only exhilarated but thoroughly justified.

A couple of days later Doc's former nemesis, gravel-voiced Gen. Lewie Merritt, flew up from Roi on a surprise visit to hear about our

Ponape victory in person. The colonel in command of Group 22 hosted him in his quarters that evening and Doc was invited to tell the story. The general listened intently, and when it was finished he shook Skipper's hand. "Doc," he said, "you shot down the first Jap plane in the Central Pacific campaign and to show my appreciation I'm going to send you and your people a case of Scotch whiskey."

The group commander jumped in. "Why general, that's mighty nice of you! The Group has a transport flight to and from Roi every day and you can put it aboard our PV whenever you're ready."

Little banty-rooster Lewie turned to him and fixed him with a cold stare. "You think I'm crazy, Colonel?" he growled. "That case of Scotch is for Major Everton and his boys and I want to know he gets it. I'm sending it to him by personal courier."

Next morning the general told us we were about to undertake another assignment in addition to base defense and bomber escort. With other Corsair squadrons based on Roi, Majuro and Makin, also with VMF-422, recently arrived at Engebi with new planes and pilots to replace those lost on the Tarawa-Funafuti flight, we'd be attacking those islands within the Marshalls group which had been by-passed and cut off by the Flintlock offensive. In the next months these doubly-dangerous neutralization raids would take precedence over our other duties. We'd still fly air patrol over Eniwetok and go with the B-25s down to Ponape, but our Corsairs were to be equipped with home-made bomb racks and on these Marshalls strikes we'd be doing the bombing ourselves.

Our center-line "field mod" ordnance racks, which Barrett Tillman in his book *Corsair* describes as the most useful tactical innovation of the Central Pacific War, were another example of spur-of-the-moment Yankee ingenuity. Designed by ordnance chief George Garner and welded to his specifications by our engineering department, they were spindly but sturdy contraptions made up of steel pipe purloined from a Seabee supply dump. Doc, who had flown a dive bomber in the battle of Midway before transferring to fighters at Guadalcanal, had the first experimental model to emerge from the workshop mounted on his "Dolores" and he was in the cockpit waiting impatiently to fire up while the Boom Room crew was still tightening the undercarriage bolts.

"Hey Major, don't you want to wait for a bomb?" some joker yelled at him.

He grinned and yelled back, "Let's see how it flies without one first!"

A few minutes later he took it up to altitude where he tested it in a series of violent maneuvers, ending up with a 70 degree power dive. The grin was still there when he landed. That afternoon he took off with a 1000-pound bomb and dropped it dead center on a target-designated section of reef across the lagoon. Returning from that flight, he climbed down off the wing, shook hands with George Garner and ordered him to take his people off whatever they were doing and put his bomb rack into the fastest possible assembly line production.

1st Lt. Andrew Jones, USMCR, with Corsair #55, "The Sudden Jerk."

The second Japanese air attack on Engebi occurred a few nights later, shortly after midnight of April 14. The warning siren wailed, we piled out of our tent with considerably more dispatch than we had the month before and sat close around our foxhole cursing a repeat-performance cloudless sky and full moon. Suddenly we saw a wispy orange thread of flame descending toward the horizon far off in the southwest. "That's the other team," Z.O. exclaimed, "let's get underground." We scrambled down into the hole.

It was a very different story this time. The five-inch guns around the airstrip thundered once or twice but no bombs fell. Forty-five minutes later the all-clear sounded and we climbed out into a world as unblemished and serene as we'd left it — word was passed that the nighthawks had splashed two Bettys after the one we'd watched go down in flames, whereupon the raiding party had broken formation and fled for home.

It was another victory, a cause for rejoicing — we were getting better at this war business and we cheered mightily as three night fighters switched on their lights in the landing pattern and touched down on the runway. In the next hour, however, we learned that it was one of those all-too-common triumphs marred by tragedy. The first man to score on the flamer we'd seen had been hit by the bomber's tail gunner and had bailed out. Another, a fellow Dege and I had known at Pensacola, had been given a faulty return vector after the fight and had disappeared off the AWS ground radar screen. The first pilot, Lt. Joel Bonner, was picked up by a destroyer in the morning while every available plane in the group was out looking for the second, Lt. Don Spatz. We searched the ocean around Eniwetok for five days but Don was never found.

One morning during those days Pop Flaherty's orders to SoPac arrived. Back at Ewa I'd had news from Dad that my Red Cross sister, who we'd long known was somewhere in the Pacific, was presently writing letters and caring for patients in the burns ward of Mobile Hospital #8 on Guadalcanal. I'd bought a bottle of Johnny Walker Red Label for her in case 113 should go that way, and since Pop's new squadron was based there I gave it to him to take along. "You thirsty bastard," I said, "I really don't expect it to arrive intact, but if you can restrain yourself enough to save a drink for her I'd appreciate it. So will she. She's a good gal."

Pop wrapped it in a clean shirt and tucked it in his foot locker. "I'll guard it with my life, Available," he replied, "and I won't pull the cork until I meet up with her."

That afternoon the Skipper led us down to the strip to see him aboard a southbound R4D and cheer him on his way.

We saw another close friend off the island during this period. The VMF-422 pilot area was next to ours and Dege, Lew, Abe Lincoln and I had been spending a lot of time trying to buck up Chick Whalen who was still badly shaken by his near drowning in February. He'd flown two thousand ocean miles up from Funafuti, he'd flown Engebi CAP hops since he'd arrived; then, the morning after Pop's departure, he came over to our area to tell us he couldn't do it any more. "I can't handle it," he said, his face a mask of agony. "I can't fly over water."

I glanced at Dege who was staring thoughtfully at the ground. We knew Chick had given his problem the best shot he had — he'd tried to beat it and he'd succeeded for awhile, but now, suddenly, it had gotten the better of him. I thought of him sitting alone on the log that night at Funafuti with tears streaming down his face. I remembered standing with Noel Bacon on the Lee Field control tower watching him make his first landing in the Beast, I thought of him grabbing us on the dock at North Island the day we boarded *Bunker Hill*, of his face as he stepped off the destroyer after two days and nights at sea, battered and naked in a storm-tossed rubber raft. . .

"Come on, Whaling," Dege said, "we'll go up together like we did in Florida, the three of us, right now. We'll take you up and fly you around and bring you back. You'll be okay after that."

Chick shook his head. "I can't do it," he murmured. He turned and walked back toward the 422 compound.

We watched him go, the cocky little ball player with the swaggering strut, wrinkly smile and ever-ready wise crack, scuffing the ground now, head down in heartrending defeat.

That afternoon orders were cut for him to return to the States.

Chapter Seven

Pilots of the dozen-odd Corsair and SBD squadrons based in the Marshall Islands often referred to their raids on by-passed Japanese bastions as "milk runs", implying they were ho-hum, piece-of-cake exercises, but we never really thought of them as such; the term was one of those braggadocios we bandied among ourselves to mitigate threatful actualities — in this case, a cluster of Flintlock-battered atolls lying within a fanshaped 350-mile radius east of Kwajelein. They were four in number — Wotje, Maloelap, Mille and Jaluit — and they bristled with coastal defense and anti-aircraft batteries manned by tough, well-seasoned troops. In late spring of 1944, when the three Central Pacific Marine air groups and their attached Navy units began pounding them with everything they had from every airstrip in the archipelago, they were expected to fold up in a matter of weeks. They didn't: they dug in deeper and fought back with such ferocity that our quick-fix neutralization plans soon escalated into a fullscale rearguard campaign that dragged on for a year and a half.

Actually the CenPac war had started the year before when U.S. Navy task forces were making sporadic forays into the Gilberts and Marshalls, an oceanic perimeter containing Japanese seaplane facilities and airfields across the latitudes as far east as Wake Island. In November, 1943, while our ground forces were capturing Makin and Tarawa, the enemy frantically set about reinforcing his bases further along the east-west line to check further American incursions. Our Flintlock strategy of leapfrogging the above four atolls to take Kwajelein and Eniwetok saved time and lives, but these four active Jap holdings athwart our backdoor supply lines had to be rendered ineffective, which is to say pulverized and/or starved out. Their aircraft had been destroyed, they'd been bombarded by the fleet in passing, but they still had plenty of fight left in them. Their AA gunners were good; they had nothing to do but catch rats for supper and shoot at us swooping down on them with our milk deliveries, and when submarines sneaked in under cover of darkness to bring them new gun barrels and ammunition they gave us a hellishly hot reception.

Such was the case on the afternoon of June 27 when fourteen of us, operating from the fighter strip at Roi, came in over Wotje on a

A four-plane division in dive-bomb attack mode.

bombing and strafing attack, our third in less than a week. As we were about to discover, the island had been resupplied the night before. Its gun crews were ready and waiting for us.

First though, a word about our dive-bombing tactics — and a word will suffice because they were entirely autodidactic, begun without preparation, practise, or even much thought; we simply added a few hundred feet more to our take-off runs, lugged our half-tons of high

explosive up to 8000 feet, pushed over into 70-to-80-degree dives above the target, centered it in our gunsights, pressed the release button on the stick and hoped for a direct hit. As noted earlier, the Corsair remained rock stable in violent G-pulling maneuvers, and it performed smoothly in a dive. We now found that even standing on its nose with a heavy exterior bomb load it trimmed up well and responded sensitively to the controls, all of which enabled us to make minor aiming adjustments in descent, hold the gunsight pip steady and lay our bombs where we wanted them. The plane made the work easy, results were good from the outset.

On our previous Wotje raids we'd met negligiable anti- aircraft fire and returned to base not only unscathed but satisfied that we'd done a pretty accurate job of hole-in-one destruction. On this strike, which was larger in scale than our earlier sorties, we had good navigation and rescue support — a twin- engine PV-1 to lead us to target, take pictures of bomb damage and lead us back again, also a PBY "Dumbo" amphibian hovering in the vicinity, plus a destroyer standing by within radio range in case of a ditching at sea. Our targets were several artillery emplacements near the north end of Wotje Island's airstrip and our attack plan called for strafing these positions after we'd dropped our bombs.

Wotje Island, with its estimated 3000-plus personnel, was the easternmost of the atoll; its weapons of assorted calibers were crewed individually and coordinated from ground-level observation and fire-control stations spaced at strategic intervals around the landmass. Above-ground facilities — barracks buildings, a power plant and radio station — had been levelled in earlier raids but they were connected by tunnels in the coral and we suspected they were still operative. Nothing was certain about this ghost island, nothing showed on it, we never saw people moving around or any kind of surface activity — from the air all we saw was muzzle blasts of guns aimed up at us. So we went after the guns.

Which brings up the ultimate consideration, the most threatful actuality of all.

When the Japanese took over the atoll in the 1930s they moved the native inhabitants from their villages in the eastern end to islets in the western portion. The trade winds in this area of the Pacific are from the east, which meant the seas on the windward side of Wotje Island were high, whereas the leeward waters of the lagoon were relatively smooth. Thus if we were hit badly enough to require ditching or bailing out, our best chance of rescue was to jump or land in the lagoon and let the breeze carry our rafts away from the enemy toward the western downwind islets where we could be picked up by the Dumbo or carried ashore and hidden by natives. Above all, we were to avoid capture by the Japs. During its initial probes into the Marshalls the Navy had learned what kind of a reception we could expect if we were taken alive by these desperate and most harried outcasts of the Pacific war. There were reports by natives, we'd seen captured photographs. In keeping with the ancient traditions of Bushido, also to raise morale within their enlisted ranks while at the same time disposing of additional mouths to feed, Japanese island commanders invariably ordered the beheading of downed American airmen.

We had this very much in mind that afternoon as Wotje came into view and we strung out in a loose attack line of four- plane division . Doc was leading the first with George Franck, a squadron newcomer, on his wing. I led Doc's second section with Sparrow Little on mine. I remember watching our PV photographic escort, flown that afternoon by Navy Lt. George King of VB-144, pull away to the south as we swung into our bombing approach. Happy-go-lucky George had our intelligence officer Jack Morrison aboard as a passenger. "Pinkie" Morrison, a spritely gray-haired leprechaun who had been advertising director of the *Chicago Tribune* in civilian days, had surprised us all by volunteering to go along as an observer on this raid, his first experience aloft in a combat area — "I want to see what you fly-boys do to earn your flight pay," was his jaunty explanation.

He was about to see more than he'd bargained for.

All was quiet on the ground below as Doc pushed over into his dive. Watching him plummet through the vastness of sky I thought of Austrian skier Toni Matt schussing Mt. Washington's Tuckerman ravine, a tiny black mote against a white snowfield literally flying down the near-verticle ravine headwall. The movie footage had been shot from across the valley and from a mile away his descent appeared slow, draggy, as though some negative force within time or space disallowed such speed and was trying to hold him back. It was the same with Doc's plane — a mere speck in the empyrean dropping at a meteoric three hundred-plus knots, it seemed to be straining for more, more, still more. . .

He was halfway down to his release point when suddenly the coral slab below us lit up like a telephone switchboard and the sky around him exploded into a black and crimson inferno. The first barrage was followed by another a thousand feet lower. Holding our collective breath we watched him drop into it, disappear for an instant then miraculously reappear under it racing out over the ocean where he was enveloped within a torrent of tracers from the beach. We stared in disbelief; it seemed impossible that he could survive such a firestorm. I heard a radio transmitter click, then a hysterical voice yelling, "*Go, Skipper, GO!*"

He did: all eyes followed him as he soared away, climbing now with tracers still showering past him. Looking down at the island I saw his bomb flare in the target zone precisely where I'd marked flashes of what had looked like a twin-mount anti- aircraft gun. It could have been that or something else — in my overextended state it could have been any kind of gun in the Jap arsenal. Whatever it was, it flashed no longer. . .

Then we heard his voice, matter-of-fact and steady in our earphones:

"Make your runs steep, fellows, they're loaded today."

The radio clicked again and someone laughed, a sound less mirthful than distracted.

Ack ack bursts were reaching up for the rest of us when Franck, immediately ahead of me, nosed over into his dive. Watching him drop away, mentally counting seconds to maintain safe interval before I followed him down, I signalled Al that I was breaking off, snapped the instrument panel bomb switch to "arm" and illuminated the gunsight. At the count of seven, I rolled slightly to starboard to align the Jerk's dive slope with a gun emplacement I'd spotted near the one Doc had smeared, and pushed over into my dive.

Palming the trim tab forward, I forced all concentration on the island rising in my face, a flat pockmarked slab coming up faster and faster, ground details getting larger, gun bunker growing larger and larger in the sightrings. The Jerk began bucking and shuddering as the airspeed indicator wound up toward the red line, but there were no AA blasts around me like with Doc — I was even thinking, Hot damn, they've run out of ammunition, when a flock of gleaming orange lightpoints burst all at once out of the ground straight ahead, slow-rising at first, twirling and cork-screwing like Roman candles, then flashing past the plexiglass. Another burst, this time a covey of incandescent birds curving by from side to side — caught within this very goddam distracting hail of firestreaks all I could think was *never mind, no time for it, concentrate, keep the pip on that fucking gun* ...

Then the squeeze of the button and a jump forward as the bomb falls free. Pull back, vision goes gray, arms sag with the weight of four or five G's, eyelids tug down eliminating awareness, sensations of control, of selfhood, identity. . . then an easing as the G's subside and vision begins to clear, the sense of speed returns. . . soaring now, climbing up and out over the ocean. Tracers flit by from behind but they're not so fast and not so many going away from them, getting out of the cone, almost in the open ...

Breathe again — yeah, take a deep breath, take a look around, make sure you're still alive ...

There are two holes in the left wingtip angled up from under and behind, a couple of small caliber hits scored in passing. Staring at them, the thought occurs that if they'd hit twenty feet to the right it might be a different story. But they didn't hit twenty feet to the right ... they didn't, they hit way out at the left wingtip where they wouldn't do any harm; hard to believe, maybe, but you're not dead, you're not dreaming — you're in the air, you're in one piece, *you're alive* ... so okay, smarten up, get back to business.

We were making our bomb runs the length of the island from south to north at 5- to 7-second intervals, recovering over the ocean in a climbing turn to the left and circling back over the lagoon. When everyone had cleared the target zone, Doc led us all the way around in a three-sixty then pushed over for his strafing attack at approximately the same position from which we'd started before. Still stress-befuddled, I had doubts about this while I was nosing over behind Franck — we'd gotten away once with running the island end-to-end, but the gunners down there had been tracking us and, conceivably, they might have a better chance of nailing us on a second pass made just like the first. There was no time to ponder hypotheticals, though, for the four of us in the lead division we were in full descent and ready to blast.

Maybe because of our bombing the AA fire coming up didn't seem as heavy or concentrated as before. We had good interval, Doc was pulling away in the distance, Franck was completing his firing run directly ahead of me, and I had my gun bunker target boresighted, my converging stream of tracers curving down and blinking all over it. Then in a flash, while I was recovering and climbing for open sky, an enormous black cloud erupted from the face of the lagoon behind my tail and off to the left. An instant's pause, then voices jammed the frequency:

"Jesus, what was *that?*"

"One of ours!"

"*Who?*"

"Can't be sure, but—"

"Zehner! It was *Zehner* ... "

It always seemed to me that the time I needed to assimilate the eye-blink occurances of aerial combat was allotted on a scale of not-enough to none-at-all, and in the same instant I was trying to grasp the fact that what two seconds ago had been a living, breathing friend of mine named Bob Zehner was suddenly nothing but a pyre of black smoke I noticed that Franck's plane up ahead was going crazy — he should have been climbing left and cutting across Doc's turn to join up but he was swinging away to the right and levelling off on an easterly heading. Worse yet, he was slowing down. Then I noticed a thin black thread streaming from his exhaust ports and I realized he'd been hit in the engine — Jesus, I thought, Zehner's gone and Franck's eaten a big one!

I reduced power and lowered flaps to keep from overrunning him. I called him on the radio. No answer. Joining up on his port wing I could see him bouncing around in the cockpit like a pingpong ball. I waved my hand mike at him but he shook his head — either he was too busy to talk or his radio was out. His propellor was windmilling, his nose was high and he was approaching stalling speed. A former All-American halfback at the University of Minnesota, George had been on a couple of strikes with us but he'd had relatively few hours in a Corsair cockpit before joining the squadron, too few to know all he should about the plane's tricky stall characteristics. I gestured with the palm of my right hand to drop his nose, keep gliding speed. He nodded and pushed forward, I raised flaps to stay at his wingtip and ride down with him on the chance that I could help him land safely in the drink. My altimeter was dropping through four thousand feet as we descended toward the whitecaps some three miles east of Wotje Island.

I don't remember exactly but it must have been at this point that I began taking stock of the situation in terms of wind, wave and enemy real estate. It couldn't have been much worse; George didn't have enough altitude now to turn and make it back to the lagoon, to smooth water and a downwind drift — he'd have to do the best he could with an ocean landing. I estimated the wind at 20 knots, the seas at 4-to 6-feet, I figured that from our present altitude he would put another mile, maybe more, between him and the Wotje Island beach before he hit the water. After that, assuming he survived the ditching and made it safely into his raft, everything would depend on how soon the PBY or the rescue destroyer could reach him. If there were many communication or operational foul-ups (and there were sure to be some), the combined action of wind and sea would put him up on the Jap shore. Also, as if that wasn't enough to worry about, there were the coastal defense guns along the beach. He'd be beyond their range for awhile, but not for long. . .

Suddenly a shadow crossed my cockpit and I looked around to see Al Little dropping into position on my port wing. Craning around further I could see five or six of our planes joined up and orbiting high above and behind us. Others of the tail end division, tiny fast-slow motes spaced at regular intervals in a descending pattern, were making their strafing runs over the island. Beyond them the black cloud hung over the lagoon, AA tracers still laced the sky and, wondering how many more of us had been hit besides the ones I knew about, the awful thought occurred: *they've blown us up*!

I'd been conscious of radio chatter all the while but I'd been too absorbed with Franck's problem to follow what was going on. We three were way out here east of the fight, it was time to report our location and status. Dreading the idea, I raised the hand mike and pressed the transmit button:

"Razor leader from four zero. Franck's been hit and is without power. Razor four one and I are with him three miles east of the beach at three thousand feet. He's preparing to ditch."

"Roger, Available," came the instant reply, "I have you in sight. Stay with him and orbit his position once he's down. I'm in touch with the PV and Dumbo."

"Wilco, Skipper."

I had an immediate decision to make: I hesitated to intrude on the frequency while rescue communications were in progress but it seemed important to know whether Franck was monitoring our messages — was his radio dead or was he just too frozen in panic to respond to our calls? Only one way to find out. I tried him again:

"George, I'm here on your wing. Are you receiving me?"

Staring straight ahead, he nodded.

"Okay, buddy, I won't talk any more but we're all with you. Doc's watching you, he's got rescue coming. We'll get you out of here. Good luck with the landing."

I figured he had two to three minutes before he hit the ocean. Sweat was running into my eyes, I lifted my goggles to wipe them, took a deep breath and tried to think for a few seconds about anything except the mess we were in. For some reason I envisioned the calendar on the Roi ready room wall which I'd scanned briefly while I was suiting up for the flight. Recalling the date, I was suddenly struck by one of those cockeyed notions that occur out of the blue in such moments: My God, I thought, It's seven days past my twenty- third birthday, I'm out here in the middle of the Pacific ocean and I haven't had so much as a lousy slice of birthday cake!

My attention returned to George who was sliding his canopy open and levelling off. I moved in close on his wing, noting with relief that he'd locked and tightened his shoulder straps. He glanced over at me once, I waved thumbs-up encouragement; he was doing everything right — full flaps, wheels up, keeping his speed until the last few feet above the whitecaps. At exactly the right second he raised his nose, mushed down, took a big comber smack on his belly, bounced off it and slammed into the trough beyond, throwing a sheet of spray out ahead as he slewed viciously to a stop. *Beautiful!* Now if only he hadn't knocked himself silly on the instrument panel. . .

Pouring on power, I looked back to see him scrambling out of his cockpit. Al joined up on me at 200 feet and while we were making our first orbit around him we watched him struggle out of his chute straps, inflate his vest and wrestle his raft out of its container. The tail of his Corsair was sliding beneath the seas as his raft popped open and he climbed into it. He looked up at us and waved. My eyes on him, a yellow speck against a blue-black ocean, I reported again as briefly as possible:

"Razor leader from four zero. Franck's in his raft and looks in good shape. He's putting out dye marker."

Back came Doc's reply. "Roger. Dumbo's en route. Keep an eye out for him."

Thus began as suspenseful an hour as any of us are ever likely to live through. Franck was drifting shoreward faster than we'd antici-pated — from our orbiting vantage, Al and I confirmed that he was uninjured and functioning, but both his parachute and sea anchor which could have served to slow his drift had torn loose during the ditching and floated away.

Within minutes the PBY Dumbo arrived, dropped smoke bombs to mark the raft's position, made several wavetop trial runs and reported that the seas were too high to permit landing with much hope of suc-cess. Then we heard Dumbo call the PV and suggest he fly to the destroyer's stand-by location several miles to the south and lead the ship to the crash site. Doc, circling with the rest of the squadron high above Al and me, approved the suggestion and ordered all of us to be ready to strafe enemy shore guns if they opened up. If they didn't, we were to stay at low throttle and high prop pitch, saving fuel to get home.

Four or five minutes went by before we had our first message from George King in the PV — he reported that he had made contact with the destroyer, that for some reason it was unable to respond to the emergency and he was flying back to the site. More minutes passed. As he appeared in the distance above the sea mist to the south we heard a faint hail on the frequency — it was the captain of the destroyer saying he was coming after all and was on his way at flank speed. The PV promptly swung around and headed back south to lead him to us.

Circling with Al, I was now keeping a close eye on my wristwatch, also on my instrument panel fuel gauge — wing tanks were almost depleted and main tank registered below the half mark. My eyeball estimate at that moment put Franck's raft no more than two miles from the Wotje beach.

Twelve minutes later the destroyer emerged from the haze making good speed on a northeasterly course. Dumbo dropped another smoke bomb a hundred yards upwind of the raft, whereupon the ship made a sharp turn to port and heaved to. It lay motionless on the ocean for two minutes while the captain assessed the situation. Then we heard his voice again, still faint:

"I can't risk my ship that close to the island for one man. . . "

There was more to his message but it was garbled and I couldn't get the full sense of it — something to the effect that Dumbo should attempt a landing and rescue.

A silence followed this communication. The Dumbo pilot had tried to land earlier and deemed it unadvisable. Now the seas were, if anything, higher than before, but he made no reply. Everyone aloft watched while his PBY, at an altitude of fifty feet half a mile east of Franck's raft, made another of its cumbersome, slow speed circuits over the sea, came around into the wind, cut its engines and dropped into the water. At first impact it reared up on a swell, its engine nacelles tore out of their mounts and its hull broke neatly in half just aft of the wings. The forward section sank immediately, the after half tipped up, tail in the air, and disappeared within seconds.

Al and I in our low orbit could make out bits and pieces of wreckage on the surface, and in the midst of it suddenly, miraculously, a large yellow raft appeared. We flew low over it as it was inflating and I counted the full crew complement, six black heads atop yellow flotation jackets, hanging on and climbing into it — apparently they had it unpacked and ready before the crash and were able to extricate it when the hull broke apart. Now there were *seven* people down there waiting for somebody to do something about getting them the hell out of the ocean. . .

Al had closed up on my wing and was pointing back toward the island. Looking over my shoulder I beheld a heartstopping sight — I saw our big fat twin-engine PV low over the beach lumbering back and forth, up and down, strafing coastal artillery positions with its single puny 50. caliber machine gun. Another off-the-wall image sprang to my mind: I pictured Pinkie Morrison pressing his face against a window, staring around aghast at what we fly-boys do to earn our flight pay. What George King was doing to earn his at that moment was the bravest thing I'd ever seen a fly-boy do, and it caused me to lay out a course of action whereby Al and I would earn ours in the next minute or so — and maybe a couple of courts martial to go with it ...

The destroyer was lying inert in the water; from all we could see at 200 feet its officers were up on the bridge twiddling their thumbs. Desperate measures were in order and, to make sure they understood the urgency of the situation, I decided the first thing was to get their attention. I waved Al away to give me elbow room, switched on my gun toggles and fired a long businesslike test burst out over the ocean. Then I signalled him to come back on my wing. When he was in position I slid the prop pitch knob forward into low and began a swing around and down, turning to place us in position to make a fullspeed bow-on pass over the bridge low enough to blow the captain's hat off. If a dry run didn't get him off his butt and into action we'd — well, I didn't know what we'd do next. All I knew was that seven of our people were out there a couple of miles in front of him drifting toward the beach ...

Al had read my intention and, bless his heart, he had his eyes open and his wits about him. As we were turning into our run he pulled up close on my wing. I looked over to see him pointing frantically at the ship — crewmen were lowering a whale boat and rescue squad from davits on its port side. My guts suddenly went awash with relief, I let out my breath and broke off our run, pulling up and away.

At that point George King took over the show. He was still over the beach shooting up gun positions when he saw the whale boat tossing around in the seas looking for the rafts. He immediately flew out and guided it to the big one, circled it while it took the PBY crew aboard, then led it over to pick up Franck. That done, Doc called Al and me to come up and take our positions in the squadron. We circled long enough to see the whale boat and all aboard it safely alongside the destroyer, then we turned to a westerly heading and started the 160-mile flight back to Roi.

It was late afternoon by the time we landed. At such a distance it was not possible that Roi control could have monitored our radio talk over Wotje, but in those days news of disaster travelled on wings of its own and our entire ground contingent was waiting for us in the parking area. We filled them in briefly, then gathered in the pilots' ready shack to listen in silence while our mates who had been behind Zehner in the strafing pattern described the crash — his left wing had blown off, he'd rolled over, gone full bore into the lagoon upside down and exploded on impact. We reviewed the attack while it was still fresh in mind, reliving it minute by minute. During his strafing run Doc's starboard middle gun had been knocked out of action by a 20 mm. round through the wing — it would have torn a lesser aircraft apart but his sturdy old "Dolores" had held together and brought him home. Others of us had taken hits, none of them serious.

Our meeting was interrupted by a phone call from the Roi control tower saying George King was in final approach and, charging out of the ready shack, we saw what looked like the whole island garrison jammed up along the edges of the runway. A cheer from a thousand throats arose as the PV touched down and rolled to a stop. First to emerge from it was Jack Morrison, ashen-faced and obviously in a

Morning after George Franck (left) was rescued off Wotje, for which Doc (center) put George King (right) in for a Navy Cross.

hurry. We of 113 crowded around him. With a rueful grin he said, "Outa my way, boys, I've gotta go change my underwear."

George followed his flight crew out and another cheer went up as he stepped to the ground, turned and closed the hatch. We backed away to let Doc speak for us. The two shook hands and exchanged a few pleasantries. I recall experiencing a twinge of disappointment — I suppose I expected a few well- chosen and heroically memorable words to pass between them, but I should have known better; they simply walked off the field together and left us standing there while the crowd dispersed.

Doc wrote the traditional commanding officer's letter of condolence to Zehner's parents in Texas, and late that evening he sat down to finish the official report of the days activities. He ended it by expressing in his own quiet way what we all felt and wanted to hear said. His account concludes:

"Lt. King returned to Roi Island where he landed with 11 to 16 gallons of gas remaining. (He) had acted throughout with great skill, daring and resourcefulness. Had it not been for him, it is doubtful any of the seven men in the water would be alive."

Next morning he put George King in for a Navy Cross.

Chapter Eight

By this time, mid-June of 1944, the worldwide cataclysm touched off half a decade earlier by Nazi aggressions in Europe and beyond had reached its climax in an all-out Allied reprisal — the amphibious invasion *Overlord* in which more than two million troops crossed the Channel from England and launched the largest military juggernaut in history across the Continent toward the Rhine. This "second front" in Europe was intended to relieve pressure on Soviet armies that had been holding off the German thrust into Asia since 1941; it was long-expected by both friend and foe, and on our mid-Pacific aircraft parking lot we devoured whatever news of it came to hand, appalled by its size and complexity — shipborne Army tacticians coordinating underwater demolition teams and assault troops, gliders full of British commandos, thousands of paratroopers of half a dozen nationalities jumping in darkness behind enemy lines while regiments of infantry waded into Normandy beaches, overran gun positions on cliffs and fought their way into villages with names they couldn't even pronounce. The island warfare fought by our Pacific ground forces was undoubtedly as bloody as the fighting in the hedgerows of France, but at least it was done in manageable increments of time and geography. War on a continental scale was beyond our imagining.

Ironically, while we were reading readily available press coverage of the war in Europe, the largest CenPac naval campaign to date was shaping up on our doorstep without our hearing a word of it. This expedition, known as *Forager*, was to capture the islands of Saipan, Tinian and Guam in the Marianas group a thousand miles to the west. Supporting three Marine and two Army divisions were airgroups of 15 fast carriers and 11 escort carriers, plus surface ships of the bombardment units. In size it was a fraction of the armada that had gathered for *Overlord* but (as we learned later) the U.S. Joint Chiefs had suddenly made seizing ground in the Marianas top priority and they were proceeding with what forces they had: they believed that capturing and operating from existing Japanese air bases on the three targeted islands would begin the end of the Pacific war, they wanted it done yesterday, and they were counting on Admiral Nimitz's 800-ship Fifth Fleet to do it on schedule if not sooner.

The first phase of their three-pronged battle plan began at dawn on June 15 when eight battalions of Marines stormed ashore against furious opposition on the west coast of Saipan. This 13-mile volcanic stronghold was Japan's Central Pacific seat of government, and to repel our grab for it Japanese top commanders, as aware of its strategic importance as ours, committed everything they had, including most of their remaining carriers. For these it was total disaster; in two days of what was known thereafter as the "Great Marianas Turkey Shoot," our submarines and the planes of Admiral Marc Mitscher's carrier Task Force 58 shot down 476 of the Emperor's aircraft and sank three of his carriers in the Philippine Sea.

It was a route for his forces ashore too, but they contested every foot of ground by digging deep into mountain caves and fighting on day after day, almost always to the death. It took three and a half weeks to drive their shrinking numbers to the island's northernmost extremity. There, cornered and drubbed into ineffectuality, officers of flag and general rank committed *hara-kiri* while their troops leaped from the Marpi Point cliffs into the sea. When Saipan's fall was announced in Tokyo on July 18, Gen. Hideki Tojo, chief architect of Japan's Asia/Pacific adventurism and the debacle his country was now facing, resigned as Premier.

The bombardment of Tinian, phase two of *Forager*, was already underway, and the third phase — the recapture of Guam, an American base since before World War I which was taken over by the Japanese immediately after Pearl Harbor — was about to begin. Robert Moskin in his book, *The U.S. Marine Corps Story*, describes how in the pre-dawn of July 21 assault units of the 3rd Marine Division scrambled down the nets into their landing craft as loudspeakers aboard blacked-out transport ships blared The Marine Hymn over the dark sea. Eight days later, after suffering heavy casualties in ridge-to-ridge skirmishing across the island, they fought their way into the charred remains of their former barracks on Orote Peninsula. Assembled in close order formation, they blew "To the Colors" on a captured Jap bugle and raised the Stars and Stripes over Guam for the first time in two and a half years.

This brief ceremony served to proclaim that the Gilberts, Marshalls and Marianas were now under American domination, which in tactical terms meant the way was cleared for already-scheduled advances into the Palaus, Philippines and Ryukyus. The Central Pacific sea lanes had been secured.

It was a costly accomplishment; from first blood shed at Tarawa to the mopping up of Guam, Marine casualties alone were 6,902 dead and 19,471 wounded. On the plus side, it had drawn out the Japanese navy and all but annihilated its air arm.

Still, we wondered why the top brass had shifted so precipitately into high blower — why all the slam-bang rush to put a thousand miles of water and a few more islands under our control? The answer was an awesome development in U.S. strategic air capability. On October 12 the first in a steady stream of new B-29 Superfortresses landed on Saipan, and on Thanksgiving day, appropriately enough, word was flashed all over the Pacific that a hundred of them had bombed Tokyo. I think we all understood that, despite Pentagon hype, the end of the war was still a long way off, but we didn't have to be told that having a fleet of land based bombers capable of round-trip attack on the Jap home islands took us a big step closer to it.

Actually, and again without our knowledge, B-29s had bombed industrial targets on mainland Japan in June and July by flying up from India into China, but this west-to-east Asian route proved impractical and they soon began coming around the world the other way. The Engebi CAP, which we shared with VMF-422, was responsible for escorting them through our air space, and the first time Al Little and I were vectored out to meet one is another of those half-century-later scenarios that comes up fullblown on memory's screen — we glimpse a tiny glint of silver above the eastern horizon which in the next second solidifies into a speck, a diamond gleaming in an azure void, becoming dime size, growing larger, speeding toward us a thousand feet below, a four-engine behemoth with long tapering wings flying the westerly heading it had taken yesterday afternoon when it rose into the air from a factory field in Wichita, Kansas. It whips by beneath us and we dive sharply down and around to join up on it, at which point I notice that its guns are tracking our flight path — its gleaming flanks, back and belly are studded with pods of centrally-controlled, twin- and quad-mounted .50 calibre machine guns that are locked onto us, following every move we make.

I glance over at Al. By his expression I see he feels as I do about this — if just one nervous nellie in just one of those pods should panic and squeeze off a burst, the whole damn gunnery crew would cut loose and that would be all she wrote concerning the two of us...

I inhale deeply: come on, I think, calm down, nobody's going to shoot, they're only snapping in dry, practising defensive drill...

Just the same, I decide then and there that when we close with the next one we'll determine by radio contact that the pilot recognizes us as friendlies and is passing the word to his gunners.

In the following days I read what literature I could find about these birds and learned they'd had a long and trouble-ridden history — famed Boeing test pilot Eddie Allen had been killed in an early model that blew up in mid air — but most of the bugs had been eliminated and they were now coming off the assembly floors as fast as they could be test flown and sent out to us.

Half again larger than its B-17 Flying Fortress predecessor, the B-29 Superfort was a fighter pilot's nightmare. I knew that the Luftwaffe had diagrammed the defensive armament of a captured B-17 and discovered there were approach angles at which it could not bring its guns to bear on an attacking interceptor, and out of curiosity I studied the B-29 to see if it too had any vulnerable approach zones or blind corners. It didn't; no matter how we came at one — side, stern, head-on, high, low — we were always looking down four, more often six or eight gun barrels. I found myself almost pitying the Zero jockeys who'd be scrambling off their home fields to meet them.

At the peak of the Marianas buildup we were taking them through the CenPac corridor at the rate of two or three a day and, good as it was to have the Pacific offensive advancing westward, it had profound consequences for us left behind in the Marshalls. Our flight duties were as before — dawn-to-dusk patrol, bombing Ponape and the by-passed islands east of Roi — but on the ground we were adjusting to the mixed blessings of life in a rear area. A big change was the orderly and contented look of our raunchy old Razor Base — Quonset huts in place of tents, neat crushed-coral paths everywhere, an officer's club, the foxhole area overgrown by weeds and now the site of our beer parties under the stars. A rotation system was worked out whereby we El Toro originals would enjoy a week at Doris Duke's Waikiki Beach mansion which had been lent to the Corps for R & R purposes. We had concerts by members of the island's all-Black anti-aircraft unit, some of them professional jazz musicians, who jammed Dixieland for a couple of hours every afternoon in the parachute loft. Bob Hope and his troupe spent a night with us and put on a show for all island personnel.

But these diversions did not entirely offset the effects of stressful months past, long hours in the air, repetitive pressures and anxieties which were lumped under the catch-all heading of "combat fatigue" and which, in retrospect, had been coming on for some time. Since early summer Dege and I and a few others of the original group had been leading four-plane divisions, we'd all taken our share of hits from groundfire, and the dangers of letting down the collective edge were demonstrated when one of our divisions got caught in a rain squall coming back from a raid on Maloelap. Lt. Peter Smith, flying tight on his division leader in near zero visibility, suddenly noticed that the ball of his turn-and-bank indicator was stuck in a corner, his airspeed was red-lining and his altimeter was unwinding like a top — he and his three mates were headed nose-first for the ocean in a deadly vertiginous spiral. He radioed this information to the others even as he fought to get his wings level and nose up. He pulled out of the dive just over the wave tops and climbed through the murk with his eyes glued to his dashboard instruments until he broke out into open sky. Panic subsiding, he called again. And again. There was no reply. "Little Smitty" flew back to Roi alone. He was the sole survivor of his division.

The war diary is not clear on the date but it was around this time that Al Little and I flew a four-plane reconnaissance flight out of Roi which had a highly irregular denoument (it also turned out to be the last hop we would fly as the Skipper's second section). Take-off was pre-dawn because a ship had been sighted off the Wotje deepwater channel at sunset; if it followed the usual Jap procedure of entering the lagoon anchorage to drop off provisions during the hours of darkness we hoped to catch it before it departed at first light. Doc's plan was to split the division and make coordinated attacks — he and his wingman would come in low from the sea, Al and I would drop down flat on the lagoon and approach from the west.

We flew by starlight most of the way but a milky pre-dawn smudge was spreading along the horizon ahead when, twenty miles short of the atoll, Doc rocked his wings and peeled off on a north-easterly heading. I noted the time and decided to hold course for another two minutes. Timing was important: if there *was* a ship in the lagoon, we'd try to hit it simultaneously from opposite directions; if not, we'd rejoin and strafe targets of opportunity on the island.

At separation plus two I orbited twice over Rurik Strait west of the atoll, killing four more minutes to let Doc get into position for his approach, then took an easterly heading and dropped down to fifty feet above piss-on-a-plate sea conditions. The pre-dawn glow was turning opalescent and it had diffused enough to obliterate all but first-magnitude stars in the eastern quadrant. I looked across at Sparrow beside me and thought of the first Wotje strike he and I had made together. That one was in broad daylight, he'd just been assigned to fly my wing, and as we were joining up after our strafing run I looked around to see him pull up into a near stall directly over the gun emplacements at the north end of the island. We returned to Roi and I expended a heavier than usual charge of post-strike tension by backing him against the hangar wall and chewing him out. "Goddammit, Little," I murmured soothingly at the top of my lungs, "what are you, some kind of maniac? You got a world class death wish or something? I'm responsible for keeping your ass in one piece and I see you hanging up there over those guns like a stuffed pigeon! Those people on the ground can shoot, you give them another chance like that they'll snuff you sure as hell!"

In the silence that followed, steady-eyed Al nodded contritely and acknowledged his error, then I noted a grin beginning at the corner of his mouth — even on short acquaintance he knew his man and he knew bicycle-pump bluster when he heard it. He was spiking my balloon, it collapsed with a whoosh, and we both broke up in a spasm of hyena-like guffaws. . .

We had enough daylight to operate effectively as we skimmed the western edge of the atoll, charged our guns, shifted from cruise to combat r.p.m. and started our 300-knot dash toward the Wotje Island anchorage area. I concentrated on searching the mist-shrouded lagoon while Al slid away from my port wing and dropped back to give us both shooting room — we were so low on the water our propwash was whipping spray off the surface. There was no sign of a ship, nor of Doc's section which should have been coming in from the ocean side, so as we closed the island I scanned the shoreline for a promising secondary target. I was about to decide on a half-demolished crane at the end of the loading dock when, to my astonishment, I made out a group of Japanese soldiers standing beside it — I couldn't be sure but they appeared to be fishing. Talk about targets of opportunity! They were all facing in the other direction, they hadn't seen us, and since we were flat on the water they hadn't picked up the sound of our engines bearing down on them.

I was too surprised to make anything like a deliberate decision — it was a couple of out-of-the-blue ideational quick-flashes that determined what I did next. I thought of the new napalm fire jelly that had been used for the first time in history to incinerate cave-entrenched enemy soldiers in the Marianas — our Boom Room crew had brewed up batches of the murderous stuff and we'd dropped belly tanks full of it on these same men the day before. Then I thought of the sheer enormity of our recent raids — a hundred aircraft at a time, eight-squadron saturation dive-bombings that lasted over three hours. Now I had my machine guns boresighted on a dozen lucky survivors who were peacefully fishing for their breakfast without an inkling that one squeeze of a Yankee barbarian's trigger finger could send them off to join their ancestors before they took another breath.

. .

Squeeze I did: I pulled slightly back on the stick and fired a two-second burst that went ten feet above their heads. They were plunging wildly into the lagoon as I roared past the crane, and by the time Al was in shooting position they were all hunkered down behind the pier. I'm sure he knew their escape was not a result of poor marksmanship on my part, but he never said anything about it to me or anyone else. Neither did I.

Climbing away after the run we spotted Doc and his partner coming in from the seaward side and we joined them over the island as planned. In strengthening daylight at angels four we could see that our primary target was nowhere in the oceanic vicinity so we circled once, strafed shore guns on the southeast point and headed back to Roi.

In August, Corsair squadrons fresh from the Hawaian and Samoan rear areas started coming through our islands on their way to the Marianas, leap-frogging squadrons that had been in the Gilberts-Marshalls for a year or more (just as eight months later One-Thirteen, with a fresh complement of pilots, would leap-frog them en route to Okinawa). One afternoon we learned that VMF-225, which had been with us at Ewa, was headed for Guam aboard the carrier *Attu* anchored in Eniwetok lagoon. We sent a Higgins boat out to bring our pilot buddies ashore for an overnight visit. Dege, Lew and I and several others were waiting when the returning boat grounded on the beach, at which point I heard the expected familiar voice, a yell — "Hey, A.B.!" — and Gentleman Jack Butler, the virgin's downfall, jumped ashore.

In freshly starched khaki he and the others looked like they'd just stepped out of the bandbox compared to us, a comparison not lost on my old schoolmate. After a bearhug greeting he stepped back. "Jesus, Jones," he exclaimed, "you're a mess, you look like you've been in a war or something! That shirt's about to fall off you. Don't they issue clothing out here?"

Before I could reply, old Princetonian Hunter Craig and my Pensacola classmate Bobby Karcher descended on us and after more pounding and back slapping we led everybody up the hill to the transient officers Quonset. There Jack dug a bottle of Old Bushmill's from his kit and passed it around. The hut was filling with VMF-422 and VMSB-151 pilots who had friends in Two Twenty-five, more bottles appeared, and before long we were embarked on a four-squadron reunion celebration. After recessing for supper we moved it out-doors to the foxhole area. There were some good voices in the group that night and we had a lot of what passed for music on these occasions — Russ Drumm singing his famous rendition of "The Bastard King of England," Frank Grundler's version of "One-Ball Riley," others leading choruses of "Paddy McGinty's Goat" and "Who Threw the Overalls in Mistress Murphy's Chowder."

Through most of it Jack and I sat apart with canteen cups of Schenley's Black Death and talked of home. I told him about my sister on the 'Canal, brother Seaver delivering Lend Lease shipments to England, Dad at age 60 still muttering about having his WW I Army major's commission reinstated. Jack laughed about his Dad, "the Colonel," who was wearing his National Guard uniform to his bi-weekly air raid warden stints on the Rectortown, Va., town hall roof. At ease under the stars, we fell into the relaxed, almost-forgotten conversational idiom of college days:

"Did you know Lindbergh's at Kwajelein?"

"Lindbergh — as in Charles Augustus? What's he doing at Kwajelein?"

"They're calling it a tour of inspection. Actually he's flying dive bombing missions."

"Bullshit!"

"God's truth. He's a consultant to Chance-Vought, he flew one of the old birdcage U's to Lee Field when we were in operational and we checked out in it — we're lucky the damn thing didn't kill us. Anyway, he's at Kwajelein right now and the MAG-31 guys say he takes off with three thousand pound bombs under his wings and drops them in the pickle barrel every time."

"I don't believe it. He's a *civilian*!"

"Take it up with General Cushman. And they've got another new wrinkle going back there. They're dropping tins of salmon and propaganda leaflets on the Nips along with the ordnance. They call this one 'psychological warfare' — you know, blow them all to hell one minute, shower them with goodies the next."

"Jesus! . . ."

It struck us funny: we sounded less like combat pilots talking life and death realities in a war

Charlie Kimak, "The Maje." This is the day he took over the squadron from Doc Everton — the C.O.'s jeep was part of the deal.

zone than a couple of white-buck sophomores gossiping over a pitcher of beer in the Nassau Tavern. A few minutes later I caught Jack staring at me thoughtfully. When I met his gaze he spoke, his voice serious. "We're riding the tiger, A.B.," he said.

"Tiger?"

"You know the old saying — you can climb on a tiger's back and ride him, but how are you going to get off?"

I knew the saying. I didn't know the answer, though, and I couldn't think of anyone who did.

The Two twenty-five chaps had breakfast with us next morning, after which we saw them aboard the boat carrying them back to *Attu*. We got word that evening that the ship had weighed anchor at noon and cleared the channel bound for Guam.

On the morning of September 7, Major Everton called a meeting of all air and ground officers to announce that he'd received orders to turn command of VMF-113 over to Major Kimak and to report immediately for duty at Air Base Command, Forward Area. He gave it to us just like that — deadpan, cold turkey, a flat statement about an accomplished fact that brooked no appeal.

It took several seconds to sink in. We stared at each other — the Skipper turning One-thirteen over to somebody else? It was unthinkable. Hell, Doc Everton *was* One-thirteen, we couldn't imagine one apart from the other!

If it took a moment for the news to register it took no time at all for us to spot the silver lining: squadron command was going not to an outsider, as usually happened, but to one of our own, to quiet, self-effacing Charlie Kimak. "The Maje" had been an instrument flight instructor at Pensacola before joining newly-commissioned One-thirteen as Doc's executive officer. We had not forgotten that during El Toro training he'd crawled into a crashed and burning Corsair and pulled Bill Duffy out of the flames. He'd flown with us throughout the tour, he'd led several of our big strikes, he was qualified in every way for the top position: there were plenty of good reasons why we should do all we could to help him fill Doc's shoes, and the best of them was that he was one of us and had been from the beginning.

The Maje's ready acceptance was another example of the top-to-bottom solidarity which Doc had instilled in us so deeply we never thought of it while he was with us; it wasn't until he'd gone that we began to perceive the full extent of the humanity and compassion that characterized decisions he'd made in a number of troublesome instances. I think of one that involved a young enlisted mechanic who was suffering from battle-rattle and who had an M-1 rifle he claimed to have been cleaning go off in his hands, shattering his lower leg. Doc asked ordnance chief Sullivan to examine the weapon for possible malfunctions. Sully stripped it, went over it piece by piece and reported that it appeared to be in sound working order.

"I swear, tears came to his eyes," Sully told me. "He knew the kid was having problems, he knew that if the wound was declared self-inflicted he would get a dishonorable discharge. He gave me the stare — you know, like he's trying to fry an egg on your forehead? — then he said, 'Take another look, Sergeant, see if the trigger sere isn't worn or something.' I got the message; I took the rifle apart again and told him, 'You were right, Sir, the trigger sere was worn, that rifle could have gone off accidentally sure enough.' That's the way the report went in. The kid's leg had to be amputated but he got out of service with a clean record."

Doc Everton's devotion to his people paid off not only in up-and-down loyalty but in horizontal lockstep at every level. It was much in evidence among the salty non-coms he'd hand-picked for enlisted leadership — Sully and John Cates, Delmar Lewis and Nick Sheppard, George Duffy, Abie Greenhouse, Jack Carol, Al Ackerman, Fred Scroggins and my plane captain Joe Gonzales, to name a few. Some of them had served with him before Pearl Harbor. They called themselves "the airfield builders" for they had prepared the airstrips and built the facilities at Ewa, Espiritu Santos, Efate, Guadalcanal and here on Engebi, and they had let it be known throughout the organization that they would lay a strip down the mainstreet of hell if Doc asked them to. Nor did our junior ratings, the 170- odd privates, Pfcs and corporals on their first combat tour, need to be told who to vote for by their topkicks: they felt the same way to a man.

But I continue to believe that we pilots who'd flown with him felt it most strongly. Ours was probably not the same blood-camaraderie of infantrymen engaged in shoulder-to-shoulder slaughter down in the mud — we did our fighting in the sky, singly encased in machines and separated by cold clean air spaces — but Doc's grilling in aerial team-work had developed in us an interdependence aloft and a fellowship on the deck that was understated and trustful very much in his own style and as binding as any other kind. A typical example was the night Augie Goetz privately asked a couple of us to lend him two hundred dollars — no explanations were offered, no questions were asked, and since Aug was a heavy gambler we each handed over the money assuming he had to square a poker debt. When he paid us back a month later I wisecracked about the perils of drawing to an inside straight. He looked puzzled, then he got my drift and explained quietly that his year-old daughter had died of spinal meningitis and his wife had needed quick money to bury her. We would no more have doubted his story than we would have held back on the loan.

By this time, late fall of 1944, our rear area CAP and occasional bombing missions were becoming routine and we long-term pilots were spending off hours sun bathing on the lagoon beach, swimming in the coral shallows and dreaming of life in the never-never land of peacetime. Lew would go to law school, I'd finish college, Dege wanted nothing more than to plunge in off Southie's beach and swim across Boston Harbor. Al Little, scoffing at our piddling ambitions ("Somebody's gotta show some class around here!"), announced he would sail on the Isle de France to Le Havre, take the Orient Express to Venice and hole up there for as long as his accrued pay held out. Jack Duttweiler took the bait: why Venice? Al gave him his seasick Bassett hound stare: "It's the only place in the world where you can sit in a saloon all day and fish out the window."

Actually, these few relatively relaxed weeks between the Skipper's departure and our return to the States served a useful purpose, even a necessary one. An outsider listening in on our simple-minded yarnings and lunatic arguments probably would have taken us for a pack of psychos strung out beyond cure; on the contrary, our buffooneries *were* the cure, or a large part of it, for they helped put the war behind us while we slid down off the adrenalin curve and tried to rediscover ourselves in new territory. Any distraction would do, the more imaginative the better. One of our number decided to have himself circumcized, Doc LaBorde did the honors, and the patient was healing well until he woke one morning with an erection that tore out all the stitches. His howling and bleeding created pandemonium in our

Quonset hut — first aid was clearly indicated and no one knew how to proceed.

"He's bleeding to death," somebody yelled, "we gotta get a tourniquet on him!"

"Where you gonna put it?"

"Where do you think, for Christ sake — put it around his implement!"

"Not me, wise guy. *You* put it around his implement!"

Finally we picked our suffering comrade up on his cot and carried him stretcher-style back to P-La-B.

For a more representative picture of the period I envision a typical lagoonside afternoon, one of many in pleasant succession — hot, a light breeze, four or five of us drying off after a swim beneath a cloudless sky that looks like nothing has ever happened in it or ever would. The world of nature and the great outdoors is a topic of never-ending fascination for us and Hap Haspell gets it into his head to discourse upon the hunting techniques of the polar bear, including its trick of covering its nose with its paw while stalking seals on the ice.

Royce Watson balks at this. "Why," he demands, "because they smell bad?"

Hap explains it's because the bear's nose is black and it stands out against the snow.

Watso, all skepticism now, goes for the jugular. "Hol' on!" he yells in his best Pecos, Texas, hog-calling style, "hol' the-goddam-hell on, buddy! How do a dumb ole bear know what color his nose is?"

Shrugging hopelessly, Hap retorts, "He sees it in his shaving mirror, you idiot, just like you see you'll never get to heaven on good looks!"

Watso, beaming, is satisfied that he's just shot down what he refers to as "a big goddam bunch of Yankee bullshit" and rests his case.

In the ensuing silence Tom Kalhorn prevails on Russ Drumm to tell his oft-told tale about Swifty and the breast pump. Russ relishes recounting how Swifty, the town drunk in the upstate New York village of his youth, staggered into the corner drugstore early one Sunday morning and passed out in a chair, whereupon a couple of delivery boy pranksters making up the Sunday newspapers unbuttoned his shirt and suckered an old- fashioned rubber-bulb breast pump to his left nipple. He came to with a start, gazed in horror at his new appendage, jumped to his feet and tottered out of the store. An hour later an Erie Railroad watchman came upon him floundering in a drainage ditch and hauled him out, breast pump still attached. . .

Freewheeling our banter certainly was but there were a few subjects we avoided, one being the torments we were going through at night. Our "sleep disorders," to use the clinical term in vogue at the time, took many forms; we were awakened occasionally by agonized cries or by someone pacing back and forth in the darkness — one fellow used to sit on the edge of his cot and crack his knuckles for hours on end. My particular plague was pyrotechnic nightmares full of spiralling Roman candle tracers, wings coming off and whirling landmasses coming up at me head-on — all the things that might have happened in the last year and didn't. I tried to deal with it by field-stripping novelist Faulkner's bifurcation of the fear phenomenon: *be scared but don't be afraid.* Being afraid, I reasoned, was giving in to the deep and abiding dread

of annihilation, getting wiped out, becoming nothing. Being scared was the sweaty emotion that went with performing effectively after burying the dread beneath a pumped-up sense of invincibility ("it can't happen to me"), also by knowing that failing to achieve effectiveness, even faltering for a second, could make problems for others and incur personal disgrace. I reasoned further that, since being scared was an artificially induced condition, the death-dread would reemerge after the condition was no longer in effect and it would take revenge for its suppression by raising holy hell in the foggy bottoms of the subconscious — ergo, the nightmares.

I can't say my slick syllogisms did much toward getting me a good night's sleep (I discovered only time could do that) but they started me on the way to something much larger, which was a new perspec-

Foxhole party on Engebi — Russ Drumm singing "Bastard King of England." (A.J. in center wearing black baseball cap, Doc Everton facing camera on his right).

tive on myself and my fellows: I began to see in the others that inde-
finable ten-foot-tall aura of competence and self-assurance we'd noted
with such awe in the Guadalcanal pilots back at El Toro. I could see it
in the old timers of Four twenty-two, in Abe Lincoln and Watso and
Breeze Syrkin who'd survived their two-day ditching ordeal, in Charlie
Reed and the dive bombers of VMSB-151 who'd been on Engebi with
us from day one. The mark of experience was on them; like the Cactus
veterans, we'd become a brotherhood.

And so it is that today we reminisce at our squadron reunions
about these final weeks on "the rock" — they're behind us now, long
gone, and we can discuss without self-consciousness our youthfulness,
our joys and sorrows and accomplishments (former Sgt. Harold Schmitt
who recently retired from the Missouri State Police, once brought down

the house by saying, "we ground men thought you pilots were gods".)
To me, though, the truest impression of my mates in these last Engebi
days is to be found in flash photos I have of them sitting around the
foxhole area in full-throated song under the stars, canteen cups raised
high — youthful, yes, but already adept at handling life's most powerful emotions, experienced beyond their years in matters of living and
dying. They wear grimy kahki and "Marine green" scivvie shirts and
beneath their fighter-jock baseball caps their faces exude gaiety and
bravado, also, on closer inspection, a kind of raffish innocence. It is
this innocence that conveys to me the truest attribute of all which,
even allowing for inevitable tinges of latter-day sentimentality, I can
only call grace — not Hemingway's romantic grace-under-pressure nonsense but a serenity, an equilibrium, an awareness derived from walking to the edge of the abyss and coming back stronger in spirit for
having done so. My dog-eared photographs do not lie; they tell the
truth, these things I see in them were real and they were there in the
faces. Moreover, even if they were ours only in passing, if it appears
to us that the spirit shines less brightly today than it did in our Corsair years, we at least know we had it when we needed it. And that's
enough.

Two or three of our replacement pilots, recently arrived, are to be
found among the jolly choristers in those snapshots and one day one
of them approached me at the O-club while Sparrow and I were having
a beer. He was a captain who'd been an elementary flight instructor
in the States, something of an oddball, a gossipy customer who had to
know everything about everything and everybody. He spent a lot of
time hanging around Group communications to pick up off-island news,
and when he joined us at the bar that afternoon he was aglow with
excitement, obviously in possession of information he couldn't wait to
impart. He said to me, "I hear you're a pal of Jack Butler in Two
twenty-five. That right?"

I nodded.

He pulled a long face and said, "He was killed on a bombing mission over Rota two hours ago."

I jammed my fists deep into my pockets and shoved down hard to
keep from smashing his silly jaw — it wouldn't help matters, I told
myself, he's new, he's dumb, he's never lost somebody he'd known
most of his life and loved like a brother. . .

Dumb as he was, he sensed he'd gotten himself into a danger-ously unpredictable situation and he departed our presence on the double.

The last of our replacement pilots arrived toward the end of De-cember. They brought several new 33-rpm records with them and Christmas morning we gathered in the mess hall to listen to Glenn Miller's "In the Mood", "String of Pearls" and "Moonlight Serenade", Artie Shaw's "Begin the Beguine", Bing Crosby singing "White Christ-mas" and a lot of kid stuff like "Mairsy Doats" and "Praise the Lord and Pass the Ammunition". We had turkey and real mashed potatoes at noon followed by an inter-squadron baseball game and a movie that evening. Next day we were back at work breaking the newcomers in on Engebi flight operations. After a week of CAP we started taking them on bombing missions to Ponape and the by-passed islands. By that time I had found out all I could about Jack's death, notably that he'd been hit over Rota's central mountains while strafing a particu-larly troublesome gun position in the mouth of a cave; the gun had accounted for other planes before his and he'd flown into it wide open, silencing it forever. I'd written his parents a letter in which I'd held back on the details — I felt badly about this but I was trying to put the matter aside until I could visit them and give them the whole story in person, as I'd promised to do.

New Years came in with parties and went out with hangovers. Major Kimak had the Seabees building us a boxing ring and he'd asked Dege and me to organize a squadron team — other units had boxing teams, he said, and there was no reason why we shouldn't come up with one that could wipe noses all over the island. It was good fun pounding and getting pounded by the men and it helped allay the restiveness that was afflicting commissioned and enlisted ranks alike. We were all laughing over a story going around about one of our old airfield build-ers who'd gone to sick bay complaining of headaches and lower back pain. Doc LaBorde looked him over, found nothing organically wrong, then sat him down and counselled him concerning psychosomatic ail-ments — he missed his wife, he wasn't getting enough sleep, he was tired of bad food and worse living conditions, he should develope an outside interest, something to take his mind off his troubles, on and on for half an hour. After it was over and the sarge was leaving, a corpsman asked him what the doc had said. He shook his head disgustedly and growled, "He told me all I need is a piece of ass and a good cuppa coffee, and since I ain't gonna get either 'till I get home I might as well forget the whole fuckin' thing."

The last happening of importance before the nine of us original One-Thirteen pilots left Engebi typified the orderly and dignified realities of wartime logistics. Our Stateside travel orders arrived the second week in February, and while we were packing our gear word came that a landing craft was disembarking cargo for us on the beach. Half suspecting what it was, we dashed down to the lagoon and there, sure enough, was an LCT with its ramp lowered and its crew unloading upwards of a dozen cases of out-of-bond liquor. After following us all over the Pacific, the booze supply we'd bought at Ewa had caught up with us the day we were starting home.

For once the situation required no debate or even discussion: we up-ended duffels, foot lockers and hand bags, discarded the contents and repacked them with carefully- wrapped bottles of whiskey. We held out some of our treasure to distribute among our plane captains and ground personnel, and that afternoon we boarded a Honolulu-bound Army troopship, each of us loaded down with unusually heavy dunnage and wearing the only clothes we owned in the world.

Six days later we tied up at the Ford Island wharf where a year and a half before we'd disembarked from *Bunker Hill*. Standing at the upper deck rail above much noisy loading and unloading of cargo on the dock, we remarked that the Pearl Harbor waterfront had finally been cleared of war wreckage, we expressed pleasure at seeing again the palm-shaded beaches and looming mountains of Oahu, but at that moment we were concerned more than anything else with jumping ship, hopefully without creating an inter-service incident. Although we'd had a pleasant passage up from CenPac (made moreso by taking considerable poker winnings from the ship's officers), our orders stipulated travel by first available means, ship or plane, and knowing MCAS Ewa flight operations would wedge nine returning combat pilots aboard the next transport aircraft to the States — meaning five hours in the air instead of five more days at sea — our problem was getting out to

Ewa twenty miles away. The ship was departing for San Francisco as soon as reloading was accomplished, the Army major in command had denied all passenger requests to go ashore, and the problem was looming larger by the minute.

We were about to give up on it when suddenly a Marine Corps six-by came rolling up the wharf and began dropping off crates at the foot of the ship's gangplank. We stared at it, thinking that maybe our shipboard poker luck might still be running. "Well," somebody said, "do we find out if that's our ride or don't we?"

Frank Grundler and I made a dash down the gangplank and I described our situation in hurried detail to the truck driver, a master sergeant with the Ford Island guard detachment. He heard me out, then looked up at the sky. "Nice day fer a drive in the country, lootenant," he drawled. "I suggest you tell yore buddies to git their trash together an' we'll all go git some fresh air." Frank waggled a thumb at the upper deck rail and within minutes we had our gear on the truckbed and were rolling through the Ford Island gate. We'd cleared out so fast the Army major didn't even know we'd gone.

Our luck lasted all that day, long enough to see us aboard an R4D in mid-afternoon, across two thousand miles of ocean to the San Francisco MATS terminal and up the metropolitan hills to the Fairmont Hotel where the Marine Corps kept rooms on reserve for its aviators returning from overseas. I remember double checking the date — Sunday night, February 25, 1945 — and writing it on the registration form, then looking at a desk clock that read seven minutes past ten, local time — I wrote the time down too, just for the hell of it. It was snowing outside, big soggy flakes that in the heat of the lobby soaked through our kahki shirts to chill blood thinned by a lengthy tour in the tropics, but it didn't matter, we didn't even feel it — we were here, we were home, we were walking around on deep-pile carpets in a building standing solidly on U.S. soil!

Dege, Lew and I had a suite on the top floor. We rode the elevator in silence (an *elevator*, yet!), let ourselves in, snapped on the lights, walked to the bank of windows and stared out over the city — through silver motes of falling snow the panorama of dark buildings glittering with lightpoints looked to us like some incredible stage set, something we remembered from long ago but could not quite credit as real. We unpacked our duffels and drank to our good fortune in decent Ewa ship's stores whiskey. We called our families in the east, waking them to tell them of our arrival. Frank and Abe and others along the floor were in and out of the room constantly, and through it all we kept going to the windows to stare in dazed disbelief at what lay beyond.

Sleep being out of the question, we placed more phone calls through a weary but cooperative midnight-to-six switchboard operator in the lobby. She rang up Dege's brothers who lived here and there around Boston, she found Lew's girl, a Coast Guard SPAR on lighthouse duty somewhere in Maine. She was running out of patience when I asked her to ring the New York number of Vallory Willis, my old girl from civilian days who had come down to Lee Field for a two-day visit so many centuries ago.

When she rang back I heard Val's mother on the other end in a highly agitated state. "Andy, Andy," she gasped, "is that you, where are you, are you all right?"

I assured "Aunt Agnes" that I was home and healthy.

"Well now listen, Andy, I want to tell you . . . oh dear, I don't know how to, but. . well, Val was married last week and is on her honeymoon! Oh, this is awful, I hope you won't take it too terribly. . ."

The operator, listening in, started laughing and my two buddies, getting the drift of the conversation, were knocking themselves out, particularly enjoying my efforts to persuade Aunt Ag that I was not about to fling myself off the roof. It took some doing but I finally got the old girl calmed down; I wished her a pleasant day, thanked the operator (who thanked me back for a good laugh), and hung up.

Dege, still chuckling, refilled my glass and handed it to me. "First things first, Androop," he said. "Take another look out the window and see where you are."

Part Three
Old Hands

Chapter Nine

Our first morning on mainland USA broke cold and still beneath a dismal gray cloudcover. It was the last Monday in February, it had stopped snowing during the night and we could hear the city stirring far below as we heaved out, showered, shaved and pulled on our grungy old khakis and boondockers. Emerging into the hallway we found early-rising executive types with briefcases waiting for elevators; down in the lobby they lined up behind others already at the checkout windows — even keeping a tight formation and our voices low we could feel all eyes on us, a half dozen sunburned, tropically attired yokels fresh from the western seas going into the cafeteria to bolt down double orders of real eggs, real toast and bacon and coffee.

An hour later we were concluding our morning's first item of business in a military clothing store, pinning combat theatre ribbons on green winter uniforms, donning shiny-visored barracks hats and shrugging into overcoats. The proprietor chattered and skipped around us like a sleeve-gartered dervish while we fitted out, then from behind the cash register he produced an album full of photographs of returned service men wearing his merchandise — "My customers!" he cried, "veterans all, heroes every one!" He asked that we honor him by lining up under the storefront awning where he snapped us with his Brownie and gave us his blessing: "*Shalom*, gentlemen, you're old hands now. Go with God. Keep 'em flying!"

We didn't feel like old hands; standing on the sidewalk caparisoned in board-stiff overcoats and squeaky cordovan shoes we felt clumsy, self-conscious, more than a little foolish. But at least we were seasonally clad and the natives didn't stare at us. In fact *we* were doing the staring, ogling crowds of office workers swarming into buildings along Van Ness Avenue, bunching up on street corners, scuttling among honking automobiles and clanging cable cars. The spectacle was vaguely familiar yet strange, remembered yet remote, a scene from a distant world. . .

Then all at once it dawned on us that what we were seeing was our own world from time past, our own world way-back-when; we were seeing American-style business-as-usual cranking up for another work week exactly as it always had on Monday mornings throughout the

Republic — nothing had changed, the country had not skipped a beat or dropped a measure in our absence, and this demonstration of bustling normality, obviously put on for our benefit, was its way of saying *good job, fellows, welcome back!*

In that instant much of the strangeness and awkwardness we'd felt since our arrival began to leave us. Our response was a characteristic blast of gibberish:

"Hey, whaddya know — we're *home!*"

"Damn if we ain't! How do you like it, Chappie?"

"Better than a sharp stick in the eye."

"We must've screwed up and done something right for a change."

"Had to happen sooner or later. Even a blind pig finds an acorn if he looks long enough."

Our euphoria gained momentum in the next hour as we arranged transportation to our home cities and thirty days of leave. Dege, Lew and Abe signed aboard a MATS C-47 that was leaving for Boston at noon, Frank Grundler found a seat in a twin-engine Beechcraft bound for Miami. By mid-morning everybody had a ride scheduled. The best I could do was a commercial flight to LaGuardia at two-thirty that afternoon, so with five-hours to pass before a departure from the municipal airport I left the group outside the MATS terminal and took a cab back up the hill to the Fairmont.

I checked my duffel with the bell captain, bought a newspaper at the desk and called my father's secretary in New York to say I'd be at the apartment late that evening. It was snowing again, big soggy flakes that stuck to the foyer windows like fish scales. Scanning the headlines in the lounge I had the uneasy sense of having forgotten something or of some chore left undone — just more sensory overload, I told myself, too much to take in too quickly. Also the novelty of solitude; this was the first time since boarding ship at Engebi that I'd been alone for more than two minutes, day or night. I thought of the solitary sea bird that had followed us north across the Pacific all the way to Oahu, riding effortlessly on air currents in our wake — someone said it was a Laysan albatross, one of the famous goony birds that colonized on Midway. I looked for it each morning at first light and there it would be, an airfoil in perfect balance with its element, Coleridge's phantom creature, disembodied, with no need of sleep or sustenance, turning its head listlessly from side to side as though looking for its final resting place but in no hurry to find it. It stayed with us until yesterday morning when the mountains of Oahu appeared above the horizon. The moment that happened it left us without so much as a wink of its eye; it simply dipped its left wing and swooped up and away, soaring high and off to the west where it vanished among the clouds.

The lead story in the *Chronicle* was of a three-week-old coal strike in West Virginia. The second lead was a feature by an Associated Press writer with the Third Fleet at Ulithi, a deep-thinker who rehashed the Leyte Gulf battle in such a way as to prove that it was the turning point of the war. It was an interesting enough piece but now that I'd been on U.S. soil all of twelve hours it bothered me that hostilities in the Pacific were still so much easier to conceptualize than labor disputes in the homeland. I stuffed the newspaper in a wastebasket and headed for the Cirque Bar off the lobby.

The bar was empty except for a Navy lieutenant drinking a martini at a table against the wall — he looked around and I recognized Walter McVeigh, my upper class supervisor at St. Paul's School eight years before whom I had not seen since. I ordered a beer and carried it over to his table. Quiet-spoken "Quigg" McVeigh from New York was joining a destroyer escort on its first sea tour and would be going aboard that afternoon. I suggested he look up Ali Walker if his ship made Pearl. I told him about Jack Butler, he told me about other schoolmates we both knew, alive and departed. Our conversation could be characterized as desultory until he mentioned almost casually that after the war he planned to take holy orders and enter a monastery. I laughed, he smiled, but his eyes were steady on mine; astonished, I saw he was serious. "Walter," I stammered, "you mean that come peacetime you're going to turn in that blue suit for sackcloth and ashes?"

Yes, that was what he meant, and that's what he did. At one point during his Trappist induction he was required to go back into the world for a brief period as a test of his commitment to the monk's calling. He threw a party for his Harvard classmates during which, in response to their doubts and questionings, he told them that after much deep searching he had decided to return to the monastic life for good. He did that too, and at this writing the Very Reverend Father M. Bernard McVeigh is abbot of Our Lady of Guadalupe Abbey in Lafayette, Oregon.

His declaration of intentions in the Cirque Bar that morning, however, struck me as just another in a series of Alice in Wonderland incongruities that had begun last night with our first look at the city and was still going on. Before I could think of a response, he glanced at his wristwatch and stood. We shook hands. "Good luck, Walt," I said. "Good luck to you, Andrew," he said, fixing me with his steady regard. Then he turned and walked away. Such was our habit of thought in those days that I wondered if we would ever see each other again.

Groundsnow was gone and a chilly norther blowing that afternoon when I arrived at the municipal airport, checked my duffel through to La Guardia and, for the first time since buying the ticket, confronted the prospect of actually boarding an airliner and flying all the way across the country with a couple of civilians at the controls. Most single-engine military pilots rated travelling by commercial aircraft on the same pucker-factor level as going into a dog fight outnumbered four-to-one, but after a smooth take-off and a big smile from the stewardess I fell to watching the Sierras slide by two miles below while mentally splurging shipboard poker winnings on a new accordian — a big 120-bass Italian would be about right, I decided, a real ju-ju monster with ivory keys and a lot of fancy scrollwork. Half an hour later above the dusk-blue Great Plains I was casing second hand car lots near my next duty station (wherever it might be) for a pre-war Mercury convertible or a top-condition Model A Ford. Darkness descended over Kansas corn country as we flew head on into night and I dosed amid a host of pleasant anticipations.

In St. Louis a doctor, mid-fifties, came aboard and took the aisle seat beside me. Friendly and talkative, he told me he had one son in the medical corps and another with Patton's Third Army in Europe. We had a drink together. I had taken off my blouse and folded it in the overhead locker but even without uniform embellishments he soon pegged me for a yokel and began asking questions, circumspect questions that sprung from an obviously genuine interest in what to him was "the other war." Without really thinking what I was doing I started talking about the part of it I'd seen. The combat actions described were all factual, but by leaning over backwards to avoid exaggeration or any trace of heroics I realized I was making a flat-footed mess of it, unravelling a skein of incidents that, apart from the unspoken element of danger, was coming out like some kind of senseless exercise — which of all things it was not. I had never considered how to go about recounting our story to a stranger, I'd given no thought as to how it might sound to anyone who had not been through it or something very much like it, and even while telling it as truly as I knew how I knew it was wrong — true and factual on one hand and, on the other, disjointed, dispirited and just plain *wrong*. Finally, disgusted with the effort, I let it run down and stop.

It was, of course, an example of the communication hangups which so often beset service people returning to families and well-intentioned folk meaning to make them feel welcome. I was aware of having failed both my subject and my listener, but in those early days of homecoming I had no sense of the experiential chasms and psychological complexities that separate a returnee and his audience. Impatient, baffled, unsure of my own responses, I realized I had to go easy, feel my way in every instance; and after having blown this one so badly I determined that from here on I would leave the war stories to the newspaper correspondents.

At La Guardia the doctor and I shared a cab into the city and I walked into our 57th Street apartment at ten thirty that night. Dad and Laura were waiting. After their embraces, loving and effusive but groping and a little awkward after more than two years, I stood gaping stupidly around the living room as though I'd never seen it before — corridor leading to master bedroom, dining room, wall couch made up for me to sleep on this night and the thirty following it. Taking in the photographs of our combined families atop the Steinway that nobody played any more I felt my throat tighten — so much erstwhile reality, so many small, unexciting details I had forgotten which had been here all the time! Dad examined my ribbons (he seemed slightly disappointed that they weren't all medals for valorous achievement) while Laura fetched coffee, Stilton cheese and my favorite cold water biscuits from the pantry.

Dad, ordinarily an evening armchair pipe smoker, was very much on his feet, walking around the room, standing waft-legged before the ersatz fireplace, shorter and a little jowlier than I remembered him, silver hair sleeked to his skull, smiling and happy. I noticed that he kept glancing over at the rogue's gallery on the piano — five of the three Jennings and three Jones children in uniform, including the two

134

girls, Sis and Jane, in the Red Cross. Finally he walked over and tapped the one of me which had been taken at pre-flight school. "About time we got a new one, don't you think, Son?" he said. "As a matter of fact I've already arranged it. You have an appointment at Bachrach tomorrow morning at ten o'clock."

I didn't know who or what Bachrach was but I knew my Old Man's devious ways and I should have been forwarned. Having nothing else to do next morning, however, I went to the address he gave me and let a shrieky-voiced androgyne sit me under spotlights in front of studio cameras with filtered lenses and click away at me for the better part of an hour. The proofs arrived five days later, on the morning dive bomber pilot Charlie Reed of VMSB-151 arrived in town to begin his month's leave, and I showed them to him for laughs — with diffuse lighting and plenty of cosmetic touching up, my "portraits" looked less like an old hand fighter pilot than a maiden's dream in a Louisa May Alcott novel.

My protestations that evening were wasted on Dad — he thought they were fine. He ordered the one he liked best, put the damn thing in a silver frame and stood it up on the Steinway where it remained for the duration.

Charles ("Muff") Reed and I had known each other since boyhood (he called his SBD-4 "Muff Diver" and his ground crew liked the name so well they stencilled it on the engine cowling). His family was from Tuxedo Park, N.Y., and during one of our Engebi inter-squadron foxhole parties I'd asked him if he still lived there. His answer, and our subsequent conversation, went somewhat as follows:

"No, we moved to the city in 1935."

"Whereabouts in the city?"

"Fifty-seventh street."

"What number on Fifty-seventh street?"

"Three twenty-five east."

"Jesus, I don't believe it! *What floor?*

Sitting on a pile of sandbags half way around the world we discovered that his mother and two sisters were that moment ensconced two floors above the apartment Dad and Laura had moved into three years earlier!

Charlie had attended Kent School and the University of Virginia; we'd met up again in pre-flight school and had gone through Pensacola together. As for looks, Charles was a recruitment poster Marine officer — square jawed, bronze complexioned, chisel featured, with eyes that wrinkled and danced with glee when he laughed, which was often. On a stool in The Blarney Stone three blocks down Third Avenue he talked about his family — Uncle Fritz who had a piece of the city's wholesale produce action and hustled rutabagas and Casaba melons shipped over from New Jersey, his maternal grandmother who lived in the old Tuxedo Park home with a huge lawn populated by rabbits, three of which he'd fed as a boy and named Flopsy, Mopsy and Gryzbowski, a distant cousin who was writing a book about Lawrence of Arabia entitled "Buggered in Baalbek". He liked to treat the musically inclined among Blarney Stone regulars to the two songs he knew. Mercifully, he knew only one line of the first — "Sweet Eloise has a social disease" — but he knew a whole verse of the second:

> "She's got a head like a monkey
> An' a body like a frog,
> An' when she gets to lovin'
> Holler *Oh Hot Dawg*,
> Rebecca-a-a-a, get that fat leg offa me!
> It may give you a thrill, pretty mama,
> But it's mashin' the hell outa me. . ."

Old chuckling Tom the bartender would draw him another cool one, wipe down the mahogany in front of him and intone lugubriously, "Ah, Charlie me b'y, you're a darlin' man. There's only a few of us left!"

But there were more than a few Prohibition-era Irish pubs left along Third Avenue in the mid 1940s — P.J. Clark's was the best known, a favorite of slumming socialites — and we paid our daytime respects to most of them. Late afternoons we escorted my girl Marian Boyd around the tonier mid-town watering spots, usually fetching up for the evening in Tony's *Trouville* or Madelaine's *Poissonier*. Charlie had a girl too but their dalliance remained strictly clandestine; apart from an uninformative physical description ("a toothsome article") he kept his own counsel and only visited her in her apartment during the noon hour ("after she gets rid of the mad dogs and Englishmen").

The days passed idly, I did some scouting of the west side music stores and ended up buying a 120-bass Excelsior accordion, a cut below the bejewelled concert model I had envisioned but still an honest, sweet-toned squeezebox with a solid case that would stand up to hard travel. Dad and I worked out the parts to several Princeton songs during our evenings together in the apartment and I ran through our Engebi repertoire for him and Laura, neatening up the lyrics where necessary. When we finally got around to my telling them what I'd been up to this long time out of country I talked about the ships we'd sailed in, the islands we'd visited and the sights we'd seen, about the Polynesians and Micronesians, their customs and as much of their history and culture as I'd been able to learn, all the while treating our combat engagements and activities in the air as sketchily as possible. Of course I was holding back on what they most wanted to hear: I knew this, I regretted it, but I was beginning to realize that, whereas the act of dropping bombs and shooting and being shot at could be described as lengthily and luridly as the teller had hot air to waste on it, the true substance of the experience — the old question, *what was it really like?* — was, for me, incommunicable (if indeed I had any communicable answer to offer, which was doubtful). For their part, the old folks never pressed; they sat still and listened sympathetically, they honored my evasions and, hard as it must have been for them to manage a household with my restless comings and goings at all hours, they cut me plenty of slack and let me work out my adjustments to homefront existence in my own way.

Two floors above, Charlie was having problems along the same line with his three ladies and was not doing much better than I. "The gals just don't *get* it, Andrew!" he exclaimed one afternoon while we were taking our ease in the Stone. "Last night I'm briefing Ma and Edie about life on the rock when in comes Sister Madelaine in a tizzy — her hero's arriving in ten minutes, we've got to get the apartment straightened up, everything squared away. He's a heavy hitter in the business world, you know, president of the company and all that, and he's putting the rush on Maggie like he's merging her with a bank or something. Well everybody starts flying around the place straightening furniture, puffing up pillows — 'that's nice, Darling,' they say, 'tell us about it tomorrow'. Yeah, tomorrow — six weeks from next Tuesday! How do you get it across to your people?"

"I don't," I admitted. "I'd like to, but I don't think it can be done.

I tried it once and did such a bad job I haven't tried since. The whole thing is too improbable. Sometimes I don't believe it myself."

He took a pull at his beer. "Maybe the best idea is to pretend it didn't happen."

I drained mine and signalled for two more. "Maybe it *didn't* happen — did you ever think of that?"

Charlie, never much of a one for metaphysical speculation, stared at me with incredulity if not downright concern. "What are you — crazy?"

"Sure, a little. Aren't you?"

He thought a minute, then laughed. "Yeah, I guess I am, a little. I guess we all are — a little."

"The fact is, chum, ours was a nasty backwater, holding-action war, dangerous as hell but that's all. No measurable results, no sense of accomplishment, nothing to show for it like the Guadalcanal chaps had."

"How about your fracas down at Ponape?"

"That was a good moment, sure enough, but there wasn't enough of it to go around. We went out there thinking it would all be like that. We expected too much."

"Well, at least we came back in one piece," Charlie replied with his irrepressible grin, "and that's something, buddyboy. Like old Tom says, there's only a few of us left. . ."

Then one morning I picked up Dad's breakfast table copy of the *Times* and read that our B-29s had dropped two thousand tons of bombs on Tokyo in a single night attack. I thought I'd read the figure wrong, but no, I'd gotten it right — *two thousand tons of bombs!* The whole account verged on incredible: the ordnance was all incendiary, napalm and phosphorous, and this raid, unlike previous drops from angels twenty and higher, had been conducted at five thousand feet — those big birds had gone in practically on the deck over the most heavily defended target in the home islands!

Actually, the *Times* report conveyed neither the full significance nor the horrendous extent of the attack: as we were to learn shortly on arrival at MCAS Cherry Point, this first low-level mass firebombing of Tokyo by Superforts on the night of March 9-10 scattered incendiaries over sixteen square miles of the "wood-and-paper" city and turned the area into one immense firestorm feeding on itself until there was nothing left but ashes — estimates were a quarter of a million build-ings destroyed and over a million people homeless. Eric Larrabee, in *Commander In Chief*, quotes a post-war evaluation by then-Brigadier General Thomas S. Power who led the attack: "It was the greatest single disaster incurred by any enemy in military history. It was greater than the combined damage of Hiroshima and Nagasaki. There were more casualties than in any other military action in the history of the world." Interviews and on-scene inspections by service historians that began in late 1945 confirmed Power's assessment. They wrote: "no other attack of the war, either in Japan or Europe, was so destructive of life or property."

At the moment, though, all we had was the news report and that was shock enough. While we were talking it over later that day Charles summed it up in a way that would speak for many Americans when they finally had the whole story. "It'll probably shorten the war," he said, "but it sounds like a lot of explosive to dump on a city full of kids and mamasans . . . "

The morning before the day I was to report for duty I exchanged pre-dawn goodbyes with Dad and Laura and took the red-eye express from Penn Station to Washington. There I changed to a local that ran west through Falls Church and Fairfax into the rolling countryside of Virginia's Fauquier County. By this time it was mid-morning: sitting at a window with my duffel and accordion on the seat across the aisle I looked out over a valley cradling a stream bordered by greening willows beyond which rose a slope of woods ablaze with forsythia, dogwood and mountain laurel — all the glories of spring along the Atlantic seaboard. I'd almost forgotten how glorious it could be.

Leave had gone well, particularly toward the end. Three nights ago I'd had dinner in Boston with brother Seaver and his gun crew while their Army transport ship *Brazil* was doing its regular 29-day turnaround from Europe and back, unloading German prisoners and loading American replacement troops for the warfront. Then yester-day afternoon as I walked up Madison Avenue after lunch with Dad at his table in the University Club I was suddenly hit by another of those electrifying retrospections from the all-but-forgotten past — in an Abercrombie & Fitch window I beheld a display of salt water surf-casting equipment, the latest in rods, reels and lures, whereupon I was instantly transported, a boy of 14 or 15, to South Beach on Martha's Vineyard, a summer evening sun low on the combers and a half acre of bluefish slashing through shoals of frantic mullet beyond the second curl; and now like on the sidewalk, rattling along through horse-and-hound country miles from the sea, I stood barefooted and shin-deep in sand casting a lead jig far out into the swirls, two or three times, watching the silver arc of the lure and its distant inaudible sploop into the water, then *oomph*, the hit and tug, the earpounding rush of blood that attends hooking the fightingest five pounds of fish in the ocean. . . and then back to the sidewalk, charging into the store, riding up in the elevator, latching onto a salesman who responds with enthusiasm to a customer with a smattering of surf-casting experience, purchasing the basics — fiberglass rod, Penn Surfmaster reel, Ashwaway Cuttyhunk line, an assortment of tinclad jigs and plugs — carrying them uptown and stowing them at the back of a closet in the apartment—

The conductor snapped me out of my reverie with a tap on the shoulder — the train was slowing to a stop before the Rectortown station ticket office. Lugging my gear, I stumbled onto the platform and spotted the slightly stooped figure of "the Colonel" waiting for me beside the only car in the parking lot. I hadn't seen him since sixth form graduation; of course I expected to find him looking older, and he did, but his heavy-lidded smile and welcoming handshake made me feel glad I'd come. Mrs. Butler, he told me, was waiting for us at home.

Our conversation was slow at first. I asked about gas rationing, he said that as as an air raid warden he had all the stamps he could use. He told me Jack's old terrier mutt had finally died and he'd gotten a pup that looked just like it from the pound to take its place. I could feel restraint in him, a hesitation or maybe diffidence that expressed itself in long pauses. He asked where I'd spent leave, I told him with my father and step-mother in their apartment on Manhattan's east side. Looking along the tree-shaded dirt road ahead I felt again how good it was to be in the country and decided to come right out and say so. "I'm not much of a city boy," I said, "I'm really very happy to be here."

Mr. Butler, eyes on the road, smiled. "We're very happy to have you, Andy," he replied.

Georgia was waiting in the door of their 150-year-old farm house as we turned into the driveway. Some tension here; a slight, still beautiful lady of powerful emotions, she put her arms around me and clung to me silently for several seconds during which I could feel her struggling to hold back tears. "Oh Andy," she said at last, "thank you for coming. We've. . .we've. . ." Her voice failed her, she turned away and led us into the living room immediately inside the entrance.

It was a large wood-panelled room with book cases on three walls, Currier & Ives prints, a comfortable, hunting country feel to it. Mr. Butler crossed to a sideboard and Georgia, regaining control, made small talk while we waited for him to come back carrying a half-full bottle of John Jameson Irish. "This was Jack's," he said, "I was holding it for his return." He set out three tumblers for what was clearly a ceremony the two had planned in advance. He poured a shot in each tumbler, handed them around and hoisted his. "Now we'll have a drink to him. Georgia and I feel he is always right here with us in the house ..."

To one who had known him the sense of his presence was strong, but in the quiet, accepting way they lived with it there was nothing maudlin or oppressive. Two photographs of him were in evidence, one in uniform on the mantel over the fireplace, the other on a table before the bay window. In this second, a much earlier one, he was in jodphurs mounted on a big gray hunter — the characteristic wise-ass Butler grin on his face made me think of him sitting in a jeep in an Oahu cane field discoursing on the properties of a boar pig's procreative apparatus and I was hard put to stifle a guffaw. We clinked glasses, drank, and followed Georgia into the dining room.

Over lunch I told them about our evening with Ali Walker and the poker game with the admirals, I told them about the foxhole party the night before he sailed for Guam, and then I recounted all I knew of his last flight over Rota Island in the Marianas, emphasizing what I thought most important about it. "By that time our squadron was stuck back in a rear area," I said. "He was up front carrying the war to the Japs, he was right up there on the cutting edge, in front of the action. I can tell you in all truthfulness that that was where he wanted to be. He told me so that night. I'm sure he'd want you to know it and I hope you can take some satisfaction from it."

"We can," said the Colonel, who had not spoken since we'd seated ourselves at the table. "We can take satisfaction and we can take pride."

"He'd want you to have that too," I said.

Georgia indicated the ribbons on my blouse. "Are those the same ones he'd be wearing?" she asked.

"The very same," I replied. "I'll go to the Cherry Point PX tomorrow and send you a set."

After lunch she took me to see his bedroom, kept as he'd left it, then we walked out onto a terrace overlooking a stretch of lawn with an orchard beyond a stone wall. Suddenly she put her hand on my arm and said, "Andy, do you think the Japs went through his pockets?"

It took me a couple of seconds to grasp her utterly preposterous question — no one who had not seen it could possibly conceive an obliteration like that of a bomb-carrying Corsair diving wide open at full low pitch into the ground and, since I lacked the inner resources or whatever it would take to describe it to her, she had to be satisfied with a simple no for an answer. It was another sorry instance of the void between those who had been there and those who had not and I ducked it by turning the talk to a number of capers he and I had been involved in at school and college. Some of them she'd heard from Jack himself, but it was clear that his versions differed widely from mine as to who did what to whom and her eyes lit with pleasure as we tried, not altogether seriously, to get the facts straightened out. A slapstick second-story yarn that had to do with one of Gentleman Jack's amatory conquests caused her to throw back her head and shriek like a banshee. For all her passion and intensity, Jack's mother had a sense of humor that bordered delightfully on the raunchy.

I had a return ticket to Washington and was planning to catch a mid-afternoon train but Mr. Butler said he had to drive up to the city for a meeting and would be happy to drop me off at Union Station. I very much doubted that he had any meeting to attend, but in her presence he always let Georgia direct the conversation and I suspected he wanted to get off on his own and talk some more about Jack.

He did so most of the way; his discourse was easy on the surface but it was freighted still with pauses, hesitations that I recognized now as expressions of his inexpressible sorrow. I realized how much strain he had been under since my arrival; the visit had been a trial for him yet I could tell he was oddly grateful for it, maybe even relieved by it — there were resonances in his voice that had not been there before.

As he rambled on I found myself mulling Jack's comments that last night on Engebi. He had climbed on the tiger's back and ridden it to the very end, and if I'd done anything at all to help him rest quietly in his father's mind I knew the trip to Rectortown had been worth the effort a hundred times over.

The Colonel dropped me at the curb before the station entrance, we shook hands and exchanged waves as he drove away. With two hours to boarding time I headed for the bar off the main concourse. The leave had gone well, I reflected once more, a pleasant sojourn and a reminder of the past that projected forward into what lay ahead some day hopefully not too far off. Right now, though, it would be good to get back to the ordered life of airplanes and flight sched-ules . . .

Chapter Ten

The Marine Corps Air Station at Cherry Point is located on a vast reserve of coastal Carolina swampland fronting on the Neuse River and encircled on its ocean flank by the Hatteras outer banks. By 1945 the Corps had achieved its wartime peak air strength of 32 groups comprised of 135 squadrons and "the Point" was headquarters of Marine air activity in the eastern half of the country, also the hub of half a dozen operational training fields inland and along the coast. On April 2 — the Monday after April Fool's day and Easter Sunday and three days after Abe, Dege, Lew and I checked into the transient officer BOQ — bulletins were posted announcing that our 1st and 6th Divisions with two Army divisions were presently establishing a beachhead on an island in the Ryukyus, a mere 350 miles south of the Japanese home island of Kyushu. This operation joined MacArthur's land army with the carrier and amphibious task forces of the Pacific fleet, thereby closing the maw of the great strategic pincers movement that had opened its jaws with Flintlock and the Central Pacific offensive.

The word going around the station was that this landing on Okinawa, the largest action in the Pacific to date, marked the beginning of the war's final phase — the Japs were on their uppers, hanging on the ropes, done for. Sure, they were still sending aircraft swarming down on our fast carriers, but most of them were flown not by experienced pilots but by "come- crazies", kids with a few hours of training and a determination to die for the Emperor by crashing into American flight decks. Our submarines were clogging western Pacific sea lanes with Japanese merchant and tanker bottoms, strangling their industrial capacity. In the nights following the first Tokyo fire bombing in March, low-level B-29 armadas had hit Nagoya, Osaka and Kobe, leaving vast areas of these major factory cities in ashes. Conventional wisdom aboard the base that day had it that our Pacific arsenal was now gearing up for the final ground assault on the Japanese homeland and that an allied "V-E Day", momentarily expected, would free whole armies in Europe for participation in this thrust into the enemy's heart, which would undoubtedly turn out to be a shoo-in.

As usual, the wise heads among us were long on speculation and short on facts. At top-secret intelligence levels it was known that, whereas the enemy's air and sea forces were indeed on their last legs, its armies still numbered upwards of five million men, a million and a half of which were entrenched on the home islands and pledged to fight to the very end in their defense. Dissension had erupted among our ranking strategists as to whether an invasion should even be attempted — some held that a total blockade of Japan would be enough to end hostilities on U.S. terms — but pro-invasion voices were prevailing and two plans for it had already been drafted: the first, in November, would be on Kyushu; the second, in March, 1946, on Honshu. Ten Army divisions would go ashore in the first landing, all six Marine divisions and three air wings would be committed. We recent combat returnees were sure there was still a lot of war ahead of us, but, lacking access to high level deliberations or statistics, we had no idea of its shape or size — that, for instance, Intelligence was estimating American casualties at a minimum of 100,000 dead and wounded. The top brass knew well that the last battle of the Pacific war would be far from a shoo-in; it would be the biggest and bloodiest of all.

Next morning the four of us were summoned to the administration building where a tense, wary-eyed 1st lieutenant in group operations handed us our new duty assignments:

Degan and Cunningham to the air-infantry training school at Marine Corps Barracks, Quantico, Virginia.

Lincoln and Jones to the operational training squadron at MCAS Congaree, Columbia, South Carolina.

This came as a blow; we had assumed we'd all be assigned to an operational fighter training base and we registered strong objections to being split up. The lieutenant pointed out that the Quantico assignment was temporary, a six weeks course in infantry tactics for returning aviators that had been "activated" the first of the year. He'd been "involved in the program from the beginning," he told us, and he could say from first hand knowledge that it was working out satisfactorily for all concerned, air and ground.

Lew was unimpressed. "Six weeks of ground pounder bullshit!" he growled. "Who needs it? Why aren't all four of us going to an air station where we—"

"When the course is over," the lieutenant interrupted, "you two will join the other two at Congaree — it says so right there in your orders." Suddenly he flushed crimson and went up like a rocket. "You airdales don't read your orders!" he yelled. "Every week more of you come busting in here all sweated up, read a line or two, start hollering all over the place and raising hell with me. I don't write your orders, for Christ sake, I can't help it if you guys don't like six weeks in the mud!" He broke off, breathing deeply and muttering the frustrated desk officer's most fervent prayer: "Sweet baby Jesus, why can't I get a rifle platoon in a line company somewhere?"

"Okay," one of us said, "what's the drill at Congaree? How about giving us a rundown on our duty there?"

The poor guy tried but he didn't know anything about air operations so we wished him a line assignment soon and left him alone with his sorrows.

Our duty, as Abe and I would learn upon arrival, consisted of leading 6-man flights of Pensacola fighter-types through forty hours of gunnery, rocketry, combat tactics, dive and glide bombing, instrument flying, night flying, bomber escort and high altitude oxygen drill. Meanwhile, we saw our two buddies aboard a Quantico-bound C-47 and next morning we packed our gear and rode a bus out to the hustling, pint-sized airfield beside the Congaree River.

We'd had enough of BOQ life for awhile and the first thing we did after reporting aboard was visit a downtown Columbia real estate office where a woman with a ya'll-drawl thick as peanut butter showed us photographs of available rentals. She drove us out to look at a furnished garage apartment in a pine woods north of town. It was exactly right, we told her we'd take it, and she drove us back to the office where everything went smoothly until Abe penned his signature on the leasing contract. The woman studied it for a moment then recited it aloud, syllable by syllable —"Loo-ten-ant John Dub-uh-yuh *Ling-coln!*" She stared at Abe, obviously on the verge of calling the cops. "Ah de*clay*ah, Mistuh Lincoln," she hooted, "ah don't unduh*stand* you! Yoah great grandaddy's soljuhs tried to burn this town to the ground in sixty-foah an' now you wanta *live* heah?"

We were starting for the door when her face came unstuck and broke into a broad grin — we yankees were getting a taste of down-home Rebel humor. We took the lady to lunch and she helped us settle into our new digs that afternoon.

Things began to move after that. Abe, an enthusiastic and radically inventive amateur cook, bought himself a kitchen apron and slipped the local butcher a bottle of Jack Daniels sour mash. In a second hand car lot I spotted a maroon 1939 Lincoln Zephyr convertible with a V-12 engine, a real gas- guzzler, but I decided I could keep it on the road by supplementing my civilian gas ration with an occasional stop at the flight line fuel pit. Not to be outdone, Abe disappeared after duty hours the next afternoon and arrived at the apartment that evening in a blue '37 LaSalle touring coupe.

By this time we had checked our students out in the F4U-1D and were embarking on a training syllabus that was much more formalized than anything we'd known in our day. It was also less slam-bang intensive — our fellows would get in a regulated training atmosphere the Corsair experience we'd had to pick up as best we could in combat-ready squadrons scheduled for imminent departure overseas. Also, instead of being assigned to squadrons individually as we were, upon completion of training the five junior pilots and their leader would ship out to a replacement fighter pool on the West Coast where they would be assigned as a unit to a squadron already in action. With the Corps at peak air strength and the war approaching climax, the training command had put together a program which, if it lacked the zip and exhilaration of the old system, would get the job done in orderly fashion.

The exhilaration we'd known in '43 had come mostly from mixing with old Cactus Airforce hands and we regularly rounded up our people after flying hours as they'd done with us and whiled away a bit of time drinking beer and shooting the breeze in town. They were deferential at first, then curious, finally at ease and eager to hear about our exploits against the Japanese. Abe and I agreed that discussing war experiences was probably part of our tutorial responsibilities, but even here with our own kind, eager airmen who would understand the technical aspects, we found it difficult to do. It wasn't self-consciousness as it had been during leave; it was simply that combat was not over for us and it seemed better to keep sharp for what lay ahead than to rehash the dim dark days gone by.

By reason of what happened twenty-four hours later, I recall the date on which I stood my first watch as MCAS Congaree Squadron Duty Officer — it was April 12, a Thursday. Shortly before noon I stopped at the provost marshal's office, drew a Colt .45 sidearm and

SDO brassard and met the Sergeant of the Guard who briefed me on our day and night rounds. The first were mid-afternoon inspections of the kitchen, mess halls and brig. After the flight line had been secured we reviewed the squad of a dozen men who would stand gate watch and provide station security during the night. After sunset colors we made the final round of the day, a jeep circuit of the base perimeter. I took supper in the enlisted mess, watched the first half of *Mrs. Miniver* in the auditorium, did an informal check of guard posts around the compound and retired to my cot in the squadron ready room at ten o'clock. After reading for half an hour I fell asleep wondering what the drill would be if a truckload of saboteurs tried to crash the main gate.

Shortly after midnight I was shaken awake by the sergeant who was exclaiming over and over, "We got him, Sir, we got him!"

I sat up blearily. "Got who?"

"The thief, Sir!" He explained that someone had been stealing food from the commissary and that his men had caught him escaping through the fence around the field.

I pulled on clothes and got in the jeep. At the far end of the strip we came on an old cotton-haired black man, thoroughly terrified, cringing in the glare of hand floodlights held by half a dozen Marines with rifles at the ready. He was clutching a loaf of bread and a small bag of onions. He told me he was one of our civilian kitchen workers — he lived with his daughter and share-cropper son-in-law and their children were hungry. I turned to the sergeant and inquired concerning procedure in such matters. He looked surprised: "Why, Sir, we lock him up and turn him over to the Provost Marshal in the morning."

"He'll lose his job, won't he?"

"Yes Sir, I guess so."

I told the old man to get the hell through the fence and not get caught swiping rations again. I ordered the men to repair the fence and the sergeant to drive me back to the ready shack.

At dawn we drove to the flight line where ground crews were warming up engines for the day's flying. One plane at the far end of the line was jumping up and down in the chocks, its tachometer way up in the red and its propwash blowing Palmetto State topsoil half way across the county. We had women Marines clerking in the offices, also in responsible control tower and line maintenance jobs, and here in the cockpit was a young WR, her hair streaming, eyes shut tight and an orgastic smile on her face, racing a Corsair powerplant at full throttle with its cowl flaps closed. I grabbed an aileron and slammed it up and down, banging the control stick between her knees. She jumped, startled, and looked out. I signalled her to switch off and climb down. When I asked her why she was trying to burn up a perfectly good Pratt & Whitney R-2800 engine she replied testily that she was *the assistant plane captain* and was readying her machine for work. If she had admitted she was just having fun making like Amelia Earhart I'd have chewed her out about the cowl flaps and let her off; as it was, I put her on hangar sweep-up duty until she'd read the engine maintenance manual again and was ready to follow proper warm-up procedure.

Relieved as SDO at mid-day, I flew a gunnery hop with my pilots that afternoon. It was Friday, Abe had invited two girls I'd never met over for supper (he'd struck up an acquaintance with one in the grocery store and she was bringing her cousin) and I left the field early to vacuum and make the place ready. The Maroon Balloon's fuel indicator was in its usual supine position a sixteenth of an inch above empty and I turned into a self-service crossroads gas station. The proprietor in greasy overalls was sitting in a chair leaning back against the wall of his shanty inside which a radio was blaring cajun music. As I finished filling up, a cat with a sparrow fluttering in its jaws came around the corner, stretched out in the dust and commenced to chew its head off. The man looked at me and grinned: "Bird-eatinest cat I ever saw," he drawled.

Suddenly a radio newsman broke in to announce the death of President Roosevelt at a southern retreat not far from where I was standing. I froze in unbelief, paralyzed by an event that everyone expected momentarily yet which, when it happened, remained to me totally inconceivable. Franklin Delano Roosevelt, our Commander in Chief, had taken office when I was in knee pants; standing there in the hot sun with a gas hose in my hand my mind went blank trying to imagine anyone else running the country — I couldn't even think of the vice president's name. I stared at the cat walking off with feathers stuck to its face, I stared at the proprietor lounging against the wall. He shrugged. "Bin sick a long time," he said. I paid him, got into the Balloon and drove off feeling more than a little sick myself.

President Roosevelt's death had a more depressing effect than I realized at first. The initial shock lingered, reactivating boyhood memories of my Republican father inveighing against the New Deal and "that man in the White House" — the name "Roosevelt" was the only thing I knew that could move him to red-faced rage and his outbursts had troubled me deeply. As days passed the shock gave way to a kind of stressful, free-floating apathy which, inevitably, showed up in my plane handling. Returning to base from the bombing range one morning I passed the lead to my wingman, circled away from the group and, determined to shake it for a moment or two, shoved over, poured on the power and pulled up into a lazy loop. The plane soared beautifully and nosed over onto its back but, instead of easing on through into its dive, it hung upside down a second too long, the controls went mushy and the next thing I knew I was whipping around in an inverted stall, then whirling earthward in a spin. . .

I recovered easily enough but I was badly shaken. Flying back to the field I recalled with a jolt that the first thing I'd ever done in a Corsair was a loop — I'd executed a faultless and unforgettable loop on my first flight in the Beast that afternoon at Lee Field two years ago. *Two years ago!* What was going on, how in bloody hell could anyone bring off a perfect maneuver in his first hour of flight and blow the same stunt three hundred hours later? Impossible, I decided, it couldn't happen!

But it had. It had happened.

I flew hard after that; I scheduled lone hops which I spent stunting and wringing the plane out for all it was worth; I pushed myself, I pushed my students, I pushed the equipment. In quiet moments off duty I played my accordion and tried to relax, but as spring advanced into summer I was still tensed up on the ground and having trouble concentrating in the air. While leading a strafing exercise my inward vision was of a section of scrub oak forest on the Vineyard, a Woodcock "tumbling ground" where I'd watched male birds perform their aerial mating dances. When XXI Bomber Command reported that Tokyo had been reduced by fire to the point where it could be taken off the B-29 target list, I remembered that E. B. White had written about a relative who had founded a settlement house in the slum section of the city — it became of first importance to me to learn whether the old lady and her urchins had survived the holocaust (other readers wondered too: responding to inquiries, White reported that "Aunt Poo" had died shortly before Pearl Harbor). I recalled a comment Mr. Butler had made on our afternoon drive into Washington — he'd said, "After we beat the Germans we should keep right on going until we've conquered Stalin and the Russians." It had saddened me that the bitter edge of his grief had cut so deeply as to unbalance his mind. Since my own funk was less the don't-give-a-damn type than the when-will-it-all-end variety, remembering his words plunged me into despondency.

But after a while, gaining a little insight, I began to realize that, although I had no plans for my life or any idea what I was supposed to do with it, I was presently doing what I was not cut out to do on a long-term basis. If I had done it well enough early on — answering the call to arms, learning to fly, assuming the specialized warrior role — my energy and enthusiasm levels were coming down just when the last act curtain was going up. How to handle it? Only one way: push harder, get nervy again, get sharp, *push harder . . .*

My resolve put me into some crazy behavior. On a Saturday morning in July shortly after my sister returned from Guadalcanal I took an overnight liberty, flew to NAS Floyd Bennett in Brooklyn and rode the Lexington Avenue subway up to meet her at the 57th Street apartment. Though she had six years of age on me, Sis and I had always been close, and after doing two years of hard time in a hospital burns ward she seemed very much the same — high-spirited, good legs, trim and pretty in her gray uniform with red piping. Her lifelong zany streak was still intact; greeting me, she gave me a corncob pipe. "You can tell everybody it's a present from General MacArthur," she laughed.

Dad and Laura were

Sis and Admiral Halsey at Noumea.

out of town for the weekend so I took her to dinner at Tony's, during which she confided that an Air Corps colonel she'd met on the 'Canal had asked her to marry him. Was she going to? She wasn't sure: he was very dashing, married and divorced, nice guy, good singing voice, loved a good time. She'd invited him to New York for a visit — she wanted to see what he looked like in the civilian conditions they'd be living in for the rest of their lives. Sensible gal.

We did the town together that night, returned to the apartment in the not-so-small hours and, since my chariot had to be back on the Congaree flight line before noon, I gave her a bibiulous peck on the cheek and caught a five o'clock subway to Brooklyn. My car was empty except for a wino snoozing at the other end so I fired up a pipefull of the Waldorf Astoria cigar counter's finest Dunhill tobacco. Suddenly a glowering subway guard materialized before me — he had the look of a parson in the presence of unmentionable sin. I held the offending object up for his inspection. "It's a present from General MacArthur," I told him. He cocked his head, rolled his eyes despairingly, and walked on.

It was a beautiful morning, the kind that gives rise to history-making ideas, and taking off into the sunrise I swung north over Flushing Meadow, climbed to five thousand feet, turned west to line up an approach path two blocks south of and parallel to the 59th street East River bridge — my thought was to thank Sis for a pleasant evening and make up for a too-abrupt departure by blowing her out of bed with a proper welcome home salute.

Flight path established, I shifted into low pitch and pushed over into a dive. I pulled out above the river, trimmed control surfaces and, shoving on full throttle, aimed straight up the middle of the 57th Street concrete canyon at the sixth floor level. Under my nose startled Sunday morning cabbies were jamming on brakes and driving up onto sidewalks at the sight of a Corsair coming at them at over 300 knots. Seconds later I was roaring up in a swooping left wingover with the Chrysler and Empire State buildings looming on either hand like two great gleaming fish breaching out of a sea of city rooftops.

Back at angels five I levelled off and steadied course on the Amber Airway #3 beam headed for South Carolina. I discovered that at some point I had bitten through the stem of General MacArthur's pipe.

That summer a legend-in-the-making was going around about Admiral Nimitz emulating Sir Francis Drake who reportedly finished a game of bowls before taking on the Spanish Armada — while his sea battles were raging far off in the Pacific our great Texas-born admiral quietly pitched horsehoes outside his living quarters on Oahu. Staff officers dashed back and forth from the communications building to read him the latest combat dispatches. It was said that he acknowledged each one with a grunt and kept on tossing ringers.

Stories about the top brass were always hot currency within the service and they often told us more about how the war was going than bulletins from the front. Abe and I heard this one (verified by a photograph in one of the news magazines) at Page Field on Parris Island where we were taking our fellows through rocketry and close ground support exercises. As noted, he and I were resigned to going back into combat, we had psyched ourselves up for it and were working hard to have ourselves and our fellows in top operational form when the moment arrived. At the same time we were tempted to take this scuttlebut about CINCPAC playing lawn games as an indication that maybe it was not going to happen after all — we reasoned that no ocean commander, no matter how stressed out, would toss horseshoes while an engagement was in progress over the horizon if he was not damn sure he had the enemy on his knees. Could it be that the end of the war really was at hand and might become a fact before we found ourselves in the middle of it again?

With this possibility in mind we returned to Congaree — I have no record of the date but it was toward the end of July. Dege and Lew were aboard by this time and had their students well along in the training syllabus. Sis and her Red Cross friend Bea Keegan came down for a visit, on the last evening of which Abe threw a luau for the six of us on the deck of our apartment in the pines. Sis's romance with the Air Corps colonel had foundered on home ground — she didn't go into particulars but I gathered that in a relaxed setting away from the urgencies of a war environment he'd come across as little more than a loudmouth with a drinking problem.

The day after Sis and Bea went back to New York our two flights received orders to proceed to the fighter pool at MCAS Miramar, California, upon completion of Congaree training. We had only three or four hours to go and we flew the last one two days later. As I was stowing my chute in the locker shed after landing I could hear an excited voice winding up a news bulletin on the ready room radio beyond the dividing wall. I hurried in to catch the end of it but I was too late; all I caught was a buzz of stunned incomprehension from a dozen or so pilots gathered around the set:

"What's an atomic bomb?"

"Where's Hiroshima?"

"Never heard of either one. . ."

On August 9 another of these mystery weapons was dropped on the industrial seaport of Nagasaki and the following day the Japanese foreign ministry sent out feelers concerning a peace settlement in accordance with the recent Potsdam Declaration (total surrender of the Axis powers). Hard negotiations followed and on the 15th the order came down from CINCPAC: all offensive action against Japan was to cease immediately.

The war was over.

That evening I had a movie date with Frances Sloan, a girl I'd met at a party some weeks earlier. She was from an old Columbia family and her father, a judge, greeted me at the front door, led me out onto the porch and with heartfelt solemnity shook my hand. We could hear cars racing through the streets, horns blaring nonstop and cherry bombs exploding from one end of town to the other. "The city's going crazy!" he said, "in all my years I've never seen anything like it." Frannie joined us on the porch and we talked for a minute before wishing him good night. "You two be careful out there," he called as I was helping her into the Balloon. Turning out of the driveway she suggested we skip the movies and drive through the downtown area to see what was going on.

Strange as it seems, I tend to think of our experiences that first evening of peace in the world much as I think of the afternoon Sparrow Little and I first intercepted a B-29 — more varied and extensive than the single zoom-in meeting we had with that spectral behemoth in flight, they had the same rush of impressions, the same element of dreamlike implausibility even while they were happening. I'd been dogged all day by a nagging incredulousness — much as I wanted, to I could not bring myself to believe that the thing was really over and done with, that after three years astride the tiger we'd climbed down safely and walked away unscathed — and now as we cruised slowly amid the bedlam of city-wide rejoicing I had a powerful urge to jump out of the car and join the crowds snakedancing along the sidewalks. Bars were wide open, windows raised and jammed with shouting people, music turned up everywhere, complete strangers embracing, laughing and singing. Sitting beside me, Frannie was full of questions. Yes, I told her, our West Coast orders were still in effect. A point system was being set up, men with the most points would be discharged first. Yes, I had a lot of points, I'd be among the early ones. . .

I didn't join the snakedances or get mobbed by delerious revelers that night but as we drove down a tree-lined street at the edge of town we passed a church, also wide open and lighted, and I had another impulse, one very different from the first but every bit as strong — stronger, it seems, for I acted on it. I pulled over to the curb and asked Fran if she'd like to go in for a minute. The night was warm, cicadas rasped in the elms around the churchyard and we could hear the distant monotone of car horns and jubilation as we climbed the stone steps, passed through a dimly lit vestibule and took seats on the center aisle in the rearmost pew.

We sat looking straight ahead. Nothing was going on at the altar but the candles were lit and overhead lights glowed in recessed alcoves along the nave. People in the pews before us sat motionless and silent as we were, a few kneeling in prayer. After a moment there was a stir in the vestibule and a stumpy little woman trailing an orange feather boa came marching up the flagstone aisle, the click of her heels echoing in the gloom. A triumphal figure, she clattered on past the choir stalls to the organ loft, sat down, switched on the console light (I assumed she was the regular church organist with perhaps a couple of celebratory clear ones under her girdle) and began to play. She was no great keyboard artist but her enthusiasm was of the sort that carries everything helter-skelter before it and the building rumbled with a rip-snorting trumpet voluntary mixed with passages from Mozart's "Exultate", all intermingled with occasional sideswipes at Bach's "Sleepers Wake" cantata.

Uneasily, aware of Fran sitting beside me, I was wondering what had moved us to come into this place at this hour on this night when my thoughts began trending into the past, reviewing endless weeks and months of flying, reliving specific actions and incidents that seemed already to be losing their particularity and melting into one massive sprawling memory. Inevitably I thought of Butler and Duff and Charlie Prather and Bob Zehner and others who would fly no more. I thought of Val's brother Dickie killed on Iwo Jima, of my St. Paul's classmate Russ Whittlesey buried by his Marine raider battalion mates on the 'Canal's Bloody Ridge, of my Princeton roommate Walter Hughson lying dead in a Normandy hedgerow. Suddenly, without warning, I felt myself gripped by mounting rage — what end, I thought, what cause could ever be righteous or necessary enough to justify the loss of so many friends who had all their lives ahead of them? As though to mock the question, lines by e.e.cummings came to mind:

> When more than was lost has been found
> has been found
> And having is giving and giving is living. . .

Lost, found, giving, living — tears of grief compounded by outrage coursed down my cheeks. I tried to check them at first but I could not; I had known only doubt and hysteria in the last hours and now I wept as quietly as I could but openly and unashamed, and after a moment I began to experience an easing of emotional turmoil, even a kind of catharsis; with this delayed and (I realized later) desperately-awaited breaking of the floodgates, anger gradually gave way to blessed relief. Another line, origin forgotten, arose from memory: *Heaven and Hell are one place and we all go there* — we all go there, I thought; yes, we all go there and some of us stay there and some of us come back. . .

And with this first faint glimmer of what I have over the years come to think of as a post-war healing process I had an almost tactual awareness of presences around the two of us sitting in the pew — as certainly as I would have been in a flesh-and-blood encounter in broad daylight I was together again with my fallen friends in that place for a few seconds that night, each of them as luminous and alive and trustfull of the future as we all were while light-heartedly signing up for the journey; in that moment the past and present were packed into a timeless here and now and I had the conviction that afterwards, when those resplendent few seconds were long gone, I would remember that they had truly been, that they had existed in our collective cognition once and that they would be again, possibly larger and more vivid with each renewal.

Fran was looking at me with alarm in her gray eyes and I smiled at her with what I hoped was reassurance in mine. I stood, stepped into the aisle and let her precede me out onto the steps. Across the city the sounds of revelry had diminished, inside behind us the feather boa lady had settled into the heartbreaking throb of Handel's "Largo", and staring up at the stars beyond the treetops I had the overwhelming sense that all was well in the world and beyond it; I knew a calmness of spirit such as I had never known before; I laughed aloud and, for the first time in longer than I could remember, I found myself believing that peace on earth might really happen after all. I wondered what it would be like to have options again, to make arbitrary decisions which could be acted upon — *or not*: it struck me that, after three years of doing all things by direct order, freedom-of-choice had daunting aspects. For reassurance, or maybe just another laugh, I envisioned Charlie Reed expounding his views on the human experience as he had during one of our blearier sessions in the Blarney Stone. "All you need in this life, Andrew, is a few breaks," he intoned. He thought this over a moment and added, " A few breaks, and a good cut man in your corner. . ."

Three days later Abe and I drove our cars north, visited briefly with our families then took an overnight train from New York to Chicago and the Superchief from Chicago to Los Angeles. Dege and Lew were waiting for us at MCAS Miramar, others were showing up hourly — Watso, Z.O. and Augie Goetz arrived that afternoon along with a number of fellows we hadn't seen since elementary flight training. Next morning an Al Nav was posted on which several of us had been promoted to the rank of captain. We wouldn't have much time to sport our railroad tracks, though, for we were told that we could expect orders to inactive duty any day. I called Princeton University and asked the registrar to enroll me for the fall semester. It had already begun, he said, but he'd hold a place.

Our orders were misdirected or lost, of course, and days of waiting turned into weeks. We paid several visits to Laguna Beach, our old El Toro-days playground, and one night as Abe and I were walking along Coast Boulevard we heard a caterwauling interspersed with blasts of laughter emanating from a house up a side street, all of which, both noise and location, seemed familiar to me. Suddenly I had it. I said to Abe, "I think I know what's going on in there." I knocked on the door, it flew open and, sure enough, there they were — Gravel Gertie who had dragged us in off the sidewalk to drink gin and grapefruit juice the night before we shipped out on *Bunker Hill*, the retired wardrobe mistress passed out on the sofa, the English character actor with the ill-fitting dentures, the bathtub-sized bowl of spiked juice and the supporting cast of overloaded Hollywood types, everything and everybody present and exactly as they had been two years before. I nodded toward the English actor. "Last time he was the Hunchback of Notre Dame'," I said to Gertie. "Who is he tonight — Richard the Third?"

She stared at me. "You bin here before?"

"I can't believe I've been away."

"Well come on in!" she bellowed. "Hey, people, here's a coupla Army guys from the airfield! Come on in an' have a drink!"

The more things change. . .

Bill Degan, Lew Cunningham, and Charlie Reed. Laguna Beach, CA, 1945.

Our orders finally came through on a Thursday afternoon in October. I reserved a seat on a commercial flight out of San Diego next morning, then I called the registrar at Princeton and told him I'd be in his office and ready to start classes first thing on Monday.

That night the four of us took our last chow together as active duty servicemen — it was in a restaurant in town and it was no different from previous off-base carousings except that we shook hands at the end and agreed to meet up again at home in the near future. I had my next meal shortly after dawn aboard an airliner headed east. As before it was unsettling to be flown across the country by a civilian, but the sun had come up on schedule, the sky was clear, there was very little turbulence and I figured he could handle it all right. . .

L'Envoi

One spring afternoon in the mid-1950s I was waiting for change at the cash register in Phil Scharlack's hardware store in Bedford Village, N.Y., when a hand suddenly came snaking out from behind me and began drumming fingers impatiently on the counter. Turning around I came nose-to-nose with Chick Whalen, his cockeyed Irish grin as firmly in place as in our flight training days. I hadn't seen him in ten years, since the morning he'd come over from the VMF-422 tent area on Engebi to tell Dege and me that he had grounded himself and been ordered back to the States; now, suddenly, here he was, and in my surprise I grabbed him in a bearhug while storekeeper Phil and his customers stared in astonishment. He was two days back from Korea where he'd served a combat tour as a Marine ground officer — he was looking up his World War II flying buddies to let them know he'd finally gotten his head straight and was okay.

His search for me had been in our best wartime direct action style; he'd gotten my address from the Boston chaps, rented a car, driven to Bedford and was about to ask street directions when he spotted me going into the store. Still grinning, he assured me he wasn't going to let me off lightly — he'd packed a toothbrush and a change of clothes and was bearing flowers for my wife. I had him follow my car out of the village and up the hill to the 50-year-old barn Janet and I had recently bought and refurbished.

Janet Wallace and I had been married six years by this time. We'd met in 1947 when she was working with Sis at Steuben Glass of Fifth Avenue in New York and I was a reporter on the *Newark News* in New Jersey. Janny was from St. Louis, we'd become engaged the following year, and on October 15, 1949, Dege, Lew, Abe and Charlie Reed had stood up for me when she and I were married in St. Louis Episcopal Cathedral. Chick stayed three days in Bedford with us and two youngsters, a quiet time of sitting around and catching up on all that had happened in the last decade. We drank a little, played some acey-deucey, laughed over recollections (one was of my getting chewed up by red bugs after crash landing in the Florida soybean field) but we didn't talk much about the war because it seemed irrelevant to his purpose — though unspecified, it was clear that he'd dropped in on us to show us that he'd proved himself in Korea, he'd vindicated what he considered his disgrace and redeemed what he thought of as his honor. In a few days he would be returning to baseball, always his first love. He'd done some off-season scouting for the Pittsburgh Pirates before

Chick Whalen, Korea, 1955.

Korea and the team wanted him back as a fulltime talent recruiter. In his own eyes he was off and running, a whole man again, and it was a joy to share in his recovery.

Today, forty years later and two years after his death, Chick's visit stands out as one among many reunions that still keep fresh alliances formed in the early days of World War II. As recounted, that last night in San Diego in November, 1945, the four of us from Congaree agreed that we would meet again back east, and so we have, at least once a year as a group, randomly and singly, not only in the east but across the country, wherever the Marine Corps Aviation Association (MCAA) was holding its annual weekend meeting. We've supported each other through the cardinal events of our lives. We've been present at the christening of each others' children and taken vows as godparents. If we couldn't attend an occasion we felt compelled to witness in person we could count on others to be there for us — when, for instance, Jack Butler's remains were brought back from the Marianas and reinterred in the new Pearl Harbor veterans cemetery, Ali Walker met the Colonel and Georgia at the airport and stood with them during the ceremony.

I should explain that I was the only one of the Congaree four that opted for the inactive reserve when we were released from active duty at MCAS Mirimar in 1945 — the other three flew as "weekend warriors" in a reserve Corsair squadron at NAS Squantum, Mass., during the civilian years that followed. Thus it was that on June 20, 1950, my 29th birthday, I had a call from Major Bill Degan, squadron executive officer.

"Listen, Androop," he said, "I have some inside word. The Korean situation is going hot — Truman will declare a national emergency day after tomorrow and our whole group is being activated. We can fix it for you to come with us. We'll write your orders, go to work on you, bring you up to speed. How about it?"

I was too astonished to reply.

"You'll be called back in sooner or later anyway," he continued urgently. "If you don't join us now you'll end up flying the weather hop in Olathe, Kansas, for the next three years. Come on, buddy, get with it. . ."

Dege's was a very generous offer and I was desperately tempted to go for it, but as far as being called back into uniform was concerned he was postulating probabilities, not certainties. The facts of my present situation were that Janet was seven months pregnant and I'd just completed my first of three postgraduate years at Yale University. I decided to take my chances on being called (I never was).

The decision sounds like an easy one at this late date, but making it stirred up a host of dormant memories and emotions. In the sleepless nights that followed I wondered if we'd ever really made the grade as old hand fighter pilots or even gotten a handle on the myriad, crowded, reckless experiences that comprised our Corsair years. Those years were not as quiescent as I'd thought; in many long dark hours of staring at the ceiling I discovered they were still very much with us.

But I think now of the moment in which I finally gained some perscetive on them. It happened a week later when the three arrived unannounced at our garage apartment in New Haven on their way to the West Coast. We had coffee in the kitchen and Dege took me out into the gravel drive. "We've got room for you in the car," he said. "We can still work the deal we talked about. Want to change your mind?" Yes, I did — but I shook my head. Then outside, as they were turning around in the driveway and Janny and I were waving goodbye, I looked at their receding faces and I realized, actually got it through my head for the first time, that they were going back to war — they were going back to war, another war, and I knew as well as I'd ever known anything that I should be going with them. But I wasn't. I was staying behind. . .

And in that moment I felt like an old hand, a *very* old hand, at last.

They came back from that war, too, Dege to his job with an insurance company, Lew to the legal department of Grumman Aircraft on Long Island, Abe, after a broken marriage, to fly helicopters with an oil prospecting company above the Canadian arctic circle. Charlie's late grandmother had left him a share of her estate and immediately after the wedding in St. Louis he'd gone south with the birds to Florida's gentler climes ("you'll find me under the third palm tree on the left") where he eventually married and fathered two girls, the elder a state junior tennis champion and my godchild.

Our word-of-mouth information net was by this time extended in all directions far beyond our tight little group; stretched thin at times, it never broke. Somebody read in a newspaper that Breeze Syrkin, Shou Price and A.T. Graham of 422 had hitchhiked across the Pacific to spend several days as guests of the governor of Ponape — they learned from him that for all the pounding we'd given his oceanic domain we had killed not one native islander. How about Japs? *Oh, plenty of them, sah, plenty, plenty!* This word, like all items of interest, was passed over a period of time by phone, letter or personal encounter and sooner or later it got around to everybody.

Then, in the late-70s, I had an opportunity to do something I'd had in mind for a long time. As a magazine writer I was given an article assignment that would require spending some time in southern California. Janny had never been to southern California, she was eager to see it, and when I asked her to come along I had more in mind for her than casual sightseeing; I'd heard on the grapevine that retired Colonel and Dolores Everton were living somewhere near Los Angeles and that they had a son on the police force in, of all places, Laguna Beach — my idea was to show her our old stomping ground and, if possible, to find and introduce her to the one man in the Corps we of 113 would always revere above all others.

I spent two days researching my story in San Diego, then we drove up to Laguna in a mid-afternoon drizzle and checked into a motel on South Coast Boulevard. While Janny unpacked I called the police department and asked for officer Everton. I was told it was his day off. Any way I could get hold of him? Policemen and their immediate families have unlisted home phones, the duty officer said, but when I mentioned that I'd flown with his father in the war he took his feet off the desk and told me to stand by. Within two minutes the phone rang. "Sir," Mark Everton said hesitantly, "are you the one-thirteen pilot Dad calls *Available* Jones?" I said I was.

That was all there was to it. Mark put me in touch with Doc and in the next hour, while a gloomy dusk turned pitch black and the drizzle became a downpour, I stood at our room window keeping watch over a stretch of glistening, rubbery-looking boulevard. Finally a pair of headlights slowed, a car pulled to a stop at the curb and the familiar stocky figure, hatless in the rain, stepped from the driver's side. I went out in my shirtsleeves to meet the colonel on the sidewalk — I gripped his hand, looked into the well-remembered bulging eyeballs, took in the somber countenance alight now with pleasure and, behind the rainstreaked car window, Dolores smiling at me. Janny came out with my jacket and raincoat and after hurried introductions we climbed into the back seat. Settling behind the wheel, Doc told us he'd reserved a table at a restaurant in Santa Ana, a nice little place they both liked, not expensive. . .

Thinking back on that memorable evening, I can't say my old commanding officer and I picked up right where we'd left off three decades earlier on a Pacific island, but it was clear from the outset that the four of us were embarked on a lasting friendship. Doc's interest in whoever he was talking to had always been almost formidable in its intensity — it was what had most impressed a couple of nervous second lieutenants upon first meeting him in the ramshackle 113 operations building at El Toro and it was Janet's strongest impression of him that night. At dinner he queried her about our children; he wanted to know not only their names, ages and interests but to know *them*, as though he could grasp the essence of each one by asking the right questions of the mother. I listened in, furtively trying to measure the aging civilian against my memories of the 28-year-old double-ace fighter pilot — corpulent, a stodgy California homebody now, a burgher at ease in an old cardigan sweater unbuttoned down the front. But I imagined that I could sense the fire still there beneath the unmade-bed exterior, and the eyes — yes, those penetrative eyes still seemed alight with humanity, the enormous caring of the man. I recalled how he had handled the situation of the strung-out kid on Engebi who'd shot himself in the leg and I thought yes, definitely, the humanity and the compassion are there too. And after a moment I noticed something else — a grayish pallor to the complexion which I attributed to his present sedentary existence but which, in retrospect, could have been a foreshadowing of the illness that would carry him off a few years later.

The Evertons wanted to show us their home before driving us back to the coast. It was a modest house on Rainier Drive in residential Santa Ana, and as Doc snapped on the living room lights we were confronted by a montage of photographs propped up in a chair beside the fireplace, a huge plywood square on which he had mounted a cutout of the Walt Disney VMF-113 logo, a skeleton astride a diving Corsair, and beneath it, head-and- shoulder photos of the squadron's original complement of pilots. Scanning the faces she knew — Dege, Lew and me — Janny gasped in amazement: "You look like a bunch of kids!", she said. Dolores laughed, "They *were* a bunch of kids!" Pouring coffee, she described the pleasure her husband had taken putting the display together, snipping away with scissors and pasting everybody side-by-side in order of rank. Oh, and he has become a Lawrence Welk fan, she added, he just loves Lawrence Welk's music, he wouldn't miss his weekly television show for anything in the world. Nodding in confirmation, Doc showed us his collection of the maestro's tapes and offered to make duplicates for us to take back home.

The couple had been childless during the war; now they had two boys, policeman Mark and his younger brother Todd, an X-ray technician. Dolores told us about Doc's visit to the hospital laboratory where Todd was employed. It was a new state-of-the- art facility and to demonstrate its equipment Todd stood his father up before a scope — to his horror, he observed a number of tiny dark spots scattered throughout the abdominal cavity. Seeing the consternation in his son's face, Doc explained that they were fragments of a 20 mm. shell that had exploded in the cockpit of his F4F during a bomber interception over Ironbottom Sound. "Our flight surgeon got most of them out," he assured him, "but he didn't want to cut me up any more so he left the small ones in there. Also," he added with a grin, "there was some shelling going on and he was in a hurry to get down in a hole." He'd been carrying nineteen splinters of Japanese steel around in his body ever since.

Three days before while we were flying out to the Coast I'd prepared Janny for southern California by describing it as one vast outdoor nuthouse, the cuckoo capital of the country — "when you wake up in the morning" I said, "you can bet something crazy is going to happen before you go to bed that night" — and she'd shrugged my words off as silly hyperbole. It was still raining when Doc drove us back to the motel and as we turned into a shortcut through Laguna Canyon we were stopped by a police barricade across the highway. Doc rolled down the window and asked the state trooper if the road was washed out. "No sir," he replied, "the road's okay but there's a couple of hippopotamuses loose in the canyon and we can't let nobody through until they're caught."

Doc laughed. I looked at Janny. Janny looked out into the rain.

Next morning the Evertons picked us up and took us for a tour of

MCAS El Toro, a massive air base now with permanent brick buildings where the splinterville shacks of our day had stood. Its mile-long runways were aswarm with thundering jet fighters and interceptors, the most recent generation of combat aircraft in America's arsenal. Doc pointed out the monument marking the site of the original control tower, we drove past athletic fields where orange groves had crowded against the base perimeter fence. At lunch he produced a news clip he'd been saving for the right moment — it was about a mother hippopotamus and her infant that had escaped from a travelling circus and were still at large in the Laguna hills.

After lunch we said our goodbyes and started driving north to Los Angeles where I had more leg work to do on the story. I spent most of that hour in the car trying once again to match my memories of the squadron leader in the Pacific with the Lawrence Welk fan in Santa Ana. At first I thought in terms of descriptive phrases, turning them over and over in futile succession — an honest man of simple taste and style, forthright in thought and action, authentic in all things. We of his former command had wondered at times why he had never made general and we'd agreed it was probably because he was *too* forthright in situations that called for a bit of temporizing or even just ordinary patience. His eruptive confrontation with General Merritt over an escort plane for our Tarawa- Funafuti flight was an example — whenever he had to choose between the welfare of his pilots and compliance with arbitrary rulings from a superior in rank he came down like a sledge hammer in favor of his men every time. We'd heard about similar instances further along in his career; given a decision between loyalty downward and truckling to the brass there was never any doubt about which way he'd go.

Then, in one of those inspired, out-of-the-blue flashes of insight, I suddenly saw the man in the round, I beheld the individual as he really was in this latter-day context and timeframe. The key to the illumination was, of course, his devoted wife: we had not known Dolores in those early days, I doubt that we ever seriously considered that our C.O. might have an existence apart from the squadron and the Marine Corps (just a bunch of kids, Janny had said), and now that I'd seen the fulfillment of his years with her I saw instantly that any seeming diminution in spirit or stature was illusory; the calm, the caring, the undaunted way of looking at life was intact, nothing important had changed; his successes had come early, and since those successes were lifelong, ineradicable, it meant that, far from having lost anything, he had gained from his wife and family new interests and capacities and become even more his own man than before. *Authentic* was the control adjective: first and last, late and early, Doc Everton had been, was, and always would be the real thing.

I saw him once more in February, 1984. I'd been in Japan and Okinawa collecting material for an in-depth magazine feature on the Marine Corps after the bombing of its peace- keeping barracks in Lebanon the previous October. I was on my way home and, on a hunch, I called him from the Los Angeles airport. I described my project and said I'd like to have his thoughts. He told me to come on down, so I rented a car and took him and Dolores to dinner in Laguna that night.

The hunch payed off: he had a few old Marine comrades in Washington and various duty stations who could provide authoritative backgrounding that would broaden the base of the story and he let his roast beef get cold while he wrote me letters of introduction to each of them. I made small talk with Dolores and studied him while he scribbled — he'd lost weight and he had that worrisome gray pallor but he was in fine spirits and he seemed livelier than before. He enjoyed talking about the Corps, he liked hearing about my visits to Camp Butler on Okinawa and the former Imperial Navy base at Iwakuni that was now a Marine air station. When I told him I was going to Beirut the following week, however, he stiffened like a poker and treated me to the famous double-whammy stare.

"Why are you going to Beirut?" he demanded.

"Well, I—"

"The men who were in the blowup have been relieved. They're back here in the States."

"Yes Sir, they're at Lejeune, I've talked to several of them. But I still want to go look at the scene, get the feel of the country — you know, walk the ground."

Doc mulled this for a moment, then shook his head. "I don't like it," he growled. "You're a high profile journalist, a mark. You could be a top-priority target for the body snatchers and. . ."

So *that* was it: he was afraid I'd be grabbed by the Islamic Jihad crazies and imprisoned as a hostage! He rambled on, thinking out loud until he finally came up with a compromise he could live with:

" . . . You can go about your business in the city during daylight hours, but the carrier *Guam* is standing offshore and I'm going to arrange for you to be choppered aboard every night for as long as you're there . . . " I expected him to conclude with "and that's an order!", and to this day I think it took all the forebearance he could muster to refrain. (As it turned out, I didn't go to Beirut — while I was in the Orient my editor's Arab contacts in Lebanon had wired him the very misgivings Doc had expressed and urged him to cancel my trip. For scenic details I was forced to rely on descriptions of the tragedy by its survivors at Camp Lejeune.)

In June of that year Ken Geelhood and I corralled some of the East Coast 113 chaps for a reunion dinner at a restaurant in Greenwich, Conn. I called Col. Pop Flaherty at Cherry Point who flew up for the occasion and who, like Chick Whalen years before, tumbled head over heels for Janny and stayed three days with us in our Bedford barn. On the evening of the dinner we placed a call to Doc and we all talked to him in turn — Pop, Ken, Dick Dolloff, Jack Dufford and Russ Drumm among others beside myself. He promised us that he and Dolores would attend the annual MCAA meeting the following October.

Later that summer Janny and I received a formal invitation to a ceremony to be held at the Marine reserve air base in South Weymouth, Mass. — Col. John Lincoln was turning command of the station over to Col. William Degan. We couldn't make the ceremony but in September we attended a lobster cookout in Scituate with Dege, Abe and Lew and their wives and I told them the Evertons would be joining us at the Association meeting next month. A few days before the meeting, however, Dolores sent word they couldn't attend. We knew there was trouble in Santa Ana, and while we were registering for the opening night ceremonies Al Ackerman and Fred Scroggins, a couple of the 113 "airport builders" who lived near him, called us into a huddle and told us what it was — Doc had cancer.

Cancer! The mere mention of the disease has the power to divide and conquer those in its hearing, and in that moment when we should have closed ranks against the dark news it cut us off from each other, shut us up within ourselves, locked each man into his own most intimate knowledge of its horror (mine was of my mother, pale and wasted by leukemia, too weak to talk, lying in bed waiting to die). Then the usual dumb questions began, and Al and Fred repeated the even dumber answers doctors give when they haven't any real ones. I felt vaguely guilty for not recognizing signs of the illness when I last saw him, but instead of worrying about it I visualized the stocky, vibrantly healthy fire-breather in shirtsleeves that Dege and I were introduced to by squadron adjutant Smith that June day in 1943. This image was followed by another, more vivid, of him standing outside his command tent on Engebi listening to my account of Larry Johnson flying through my propwash and spinning into the lagoon — I recalled his intent face sweating in late afternoon sunlight, taking in every word, evaluating every fact, then nodding at last, dismissing the accident and asking *me* how *I* felt. Now, so long after, the question seemed absurdly, splendidly in character — his first impulse after learning Larry was okay was to buck up the guy who could not help feeling responsible — and I knew then that this was my picture of the man, the bottom-line memory of him that I would hold before all others always.

He kept his killer at bay for awhile, a couple of years, and then it began slowly to gain ground. Vic Erickson checked with Dolores by phone every week from Minnesota. Art Buchwald, on a California speaking tour, visited with him shortly before he was hospitalized. Ackerman and Scroggins faithfully kept the information net up to date. Then early on the evening of February 15, 1991, Frank Drury called from Florida to tell me he was gone, a peaceful passing with the family around him. Frank said he'd gotten the word from Vic and that I was the only one he'd told thus far, so with all the others to notify we spent the next ten minutes divvying up the dozen or so 113 names and phone numbers we had between us.

Thus began one of the most extraordinary nights of my life. First I called Vic to learn what he knew about the situation in Santa Ana at the moment, then I talked to Lew in Massachussetts and Dege who was vacationing in Florida. Next I called Joe Schellack in Tulsa, Oklahoma. I'd heard Joe was having some kind of hip trouble and his wife Mutt, who answered the phone, told me he was bedridden with a malignant bone tumor. She put him on but I was too shocked to speak — smiling, boyish Joe Schellack, youngest pilot in the squadron and top scorer in the Ponape air battle! He guessed what my call was about and in a quavery voice said, "Doc's dead, is he?" I said yes. There was a pause, he coughed several times, caught his breath. "Well," he drawled, "Well. . ."

"Listen, Joe," I stammered, "I had no idea. . . I mean, that your hip was. . ."

"Yeah," he said weakly, "it's a pain in the ass. In the hip, too."

For a couple of minutes we traded the feeble assurances that are passed in such situations, then Joe, noticeably tiring, broke the connection with a phrase we'd all been using on each other more and more, in fair weather and foul, as the years passed. He said, "I love ya, buddy. . ."

After Joe, while working my way down my call list, I became aware of a strange pattern emerging; I would state my message, there would be a pause followed by an exchange of solemnities, then whoever I was talking with would laugh abruptly and launch into something he remembered that had happened while Doc had command of 113. I forget which of our people it was who'd been in the Ewa operations office the morning one of our Corsairs parted company with the runway and exploded the squadron latrine into a cloud of splinters — guffawing into the phone, he cried, "I looked over at the Old Man and I thought his eyes would bug right outa his head!" Another of our oldtimers, one of the line crewmen, broke up completely recalling the time we took off from Roi for Engebi with a belly tank full of beer: "When you guys. . . Jesus, I bust a gut just thinkin' about it!. . .I mean, when you guys hit the turbulence and Mr. Degan looked back and there was a whole goddam tankfull of Lucky Lager blowing out the overflow pipe all over the Pacific ocean!. . ."

Somewhere during these calls I thought of the adage about a life well lived being cause for rejoicing and it struck me that this was exactly what we were doing — we were *rejoicing*, we were celebrating a life well lived, and it was spreading like a contagion; the stories, the laughter, the remembering went on from man to man well into the night, a ripple-effect of joyous recollection fanning out by phone line into the far reaches of the country.

It was after midnight when I finally finished the list. Janny had lasted through most of it but she was sound asleep when I turned out the light. Doc would have liked it, I thought staring into the darkness, he would have liked to be in on it — and, for all any of us knew, maybe he was. . .

Now it is a bright mid-morning four days later; a bumper- to-bumper line of cars and limousines nudges up a rise of ground and through wrought iron gates into El Toro Memorial Park a few miles east of the air station. Back in the body of the line Janet and I top the hill in our economy rental and start down a long stretch of lawn with grave markers on either hand. Cars in the lead park beside the dirt track, people are gathering along the slope, old friends greeting each other, smiling, shaking hands, their talk superimposed on the portentous murmurings of jet aircraft engines in the distance. I see some of our 113 men, Al and Fred, Abie Greenhouse and George Duffy; they see me, call out, "Hey, Cap'm!" A moment later former pilot Shelby Forrest enters our circle and we join a nearby group of 212 veterans gathered around retired Brig. Gen. Fred "Beanie" Payne . . .

Dolores appears walking on Todd's arm, and a group of uniformed policemen closes quietly around them — it's Mark with a contingent of fellow officers from Laguna PD. Todd sets a chair for his mother in front of the outdoor lectern, the chaplain greets her and a Marine honor guard in dress blues positions the bier beside a freshly dug hole. A hush descends on the crowd. The Chaplain waits for silence; then, bowing his head, he begins:

". . . I am the resurrection and the life, saith the Lord: he that believeth in me, though he were dead, yet shall he live . . ."

We follow the service on printed cards, mumbling the prayers and reading the psalms responsively. At one point the honor guard moves off, unstacks rifles and files silently up the hill. More prayers, a pause, then Taps sounds distantly on the morning air, the bugler high on the ridge behind us:

> Day is done, gone the sun
> From the lake, from the hill,
> From the sky.
> All is well, safely rest. God is nigh.

Another pause: commands spoken quietly up the slope, then the ragged successive cracks of small caliber rifles firing the salute. A slight trim black master sergeant ceremoniously lifts the Colors from the top of the bier, folds them and lays them gently in Dolores' lap, after which the chaplain gives the final blessing. . .

The congregation relaxes, chatter resumes at its former level, condolences crowd in upon the family from all sides. There is to be a reception at the El Toro Officers Club and a few guests start drifting toward the parking area but others hang back, continue to mill around as though waiting for something to happen. I catch Janny's eye — sure, I know, on such a beautiful day it's a shame to go indoors and all that, but this is crazy southern California and even at a memorial service we can expect the unexpected. . .

And then, so distant as to be barely noticeable, we become aware of a non-directional buzzing sound that slowly grows to a hum; the hum grows louder until in an instant it becomes a never-to-be-forgotten blast of sound, a combination whine and roar, as an F4U-1D Corsair bursts over the hill behind us and flashes low over our heads, rocking its wings in greeting. . .

We stand transfixed for a second, then, as one, we break out in full-throated cheering. We stare in astonishment, we grab each other, a babble of shouting ensues ("I didn't know we had any of 'em *left*!" — "Where'd it *come* from, for God's sake? — "Who *found* it?" . . .") as we watch it bank gracefully and turn to come around for another pass. It is in beautiful condition, its waxed blue-gray fuselage and silver underbody gleaming in the noonday brilliance. The consensus on the ground is that it belongs to a WWII aviation buff, probably an old fighter jock, who keeps it tuned up and polished and flies it to air shows around the country. . .

It swoops over us once more, pulls up in a wingover and climbs away to the west, rocking its wings again in farewell. Someone comments favorably on the plane handling — "guy at the controls knows what he's doing, whoever he is" — and the crowd, still bandying speculations, begins to move toward the cars. But the spell has a firm grip on a few of us; it lingers for a minute more and Janny stands by while I follow the plane out of sight, an infinitesimal speck receding into the depths of sky. For me, the speculations are so much wasted breath; I know who the guy at the controls is and he knows what he's doing as well as anyone who ever flew the bentwing fighter — free of disease now, with a youthful heart and a belly full of scrap metal, he's our old C.O. flying #44 off into the clouds for the last time. . .

Half an hour later Janny and I entered the El Toro O-Club, signed the guest book and paid our respects to Dolores, Mark and Todd in the receiving line. A watercolor painted for the occasion stood on an easel at the entrance to the club's reception room — it depicted Doc's F4F locked in aerial combat over Henderson Field with a Zero flown by Saburo Sakai, one of Japan's top fighter aces. As we stood beside it looking in at the gathering of guests around the floor, so many retired men and officers I'd served with so long ago, I recalled my son's remark of a few years earlier — "Dad, you were lucky, you had a war" — and I thought, Yes son, we were luckier than you can imagine and in more ways than you know, for if you apply the word (you'll learn a better one some day but this one will do for the moment) not merely to our having survived the experience or to the nature of the experience itself but to the man who led us in it you might be able to catch a glimpse of one who—

No, I realized then, he could never do that, nor should I encourage him to try; it was *our* war, not his — it was indeed a period set apart in our lives, one unlike anything we've known before or ever will again, and it was time to leave it, let it go. . .

We were unable to stay for the luncheon and as we were saying goodbye to the family Dolores took me aside to show me a letter Doc had received from "one of his boys" during his last days. Reading it my eyes went blurry as I realized for good and always that the man and the war had a part in my life I would never lose or ever choose to

The chappies fifty years later: Left to right — Droop, Dege, Abe and Lew, still enjoying life and each other's company.

relinquish if I could. I committed the end of the letter to memory. It read:

"Skipper, I feel like I'm saying goodbye. I don't usually carry on like this, but I want to say that I believe we're all going to the same place. You're going there ahead of us, we'll be on hand to see you off, we'll catch up with you in time, and we'll have the same kind of wonderful reunion we've always had. Meanwhile,

Semper Fidelis, Sir. . ."

Publisher's Message

It is a great pleasure to be able to publish this story of *The Corsair Years*. It is more than a yarn, although anytime you get a Marine, especially an aviator, to talk about their flying career it seems so fascinating to us who have never graced the skies to separate "tall tales" from true stories.

Marine aviators are a special breed and that is certainly the case of Mr. Andrew Jones, an adventurer who has lived what he writes. There is a mystique about the man and the machine which he writes about — the Corsair.

It is my sincere hope that you enjoy this part of Marine aviation history. Other books which Turner Publishing Company have released include, the following:

> *Marine Corps Aviation Association Chronology, 1912-1954*
> *U.S. Marine Corps Aviation Unit Insignia, 1941-1946*
> *American Defenders of Bataan and Corregidor*
> *Chosin Few North Korea, November-December, 1950*
> *2nd Marine Division*
> *3rd Marine Division*
> *4th Marine Division*
> *5th Marine Division*
> *6th Marine Division*
> *9th Marine Defense Battalion and AAA Battalion*
> *Guadalcanal 50th Anniversary*
> *The Battle at Iwo Jima and the Men Who Fought There*
> *Women Marine Association*

For a free catalog of more than 200 military titles or for more information, please call 1-800-788-3350.

Sincerely yours,

Dave Turner
President